This is
INDIA

This is
INDIA

Text by Shobita Punja
Preface by Mark Tully

Photographs by Gerald Cubitt
with
Fredrik Arvidsson, Norma and
Maurice Joseph and Neil McAllister

NH
NEW
HOLLAND

This edition published in 2007 by
New Holland Publishers (UK) Ltd
London • Cape Town • Sydney • Auckland

First published in 1996

16 15 14 13 12 11

Garfield House, 86–88 Edgware Road
London W2 2EA, United Kingdom

80 McKenzie Street
Cape Town 8001, South Africa

Unit 1, 66 Gibbes Street
Chatswood, NSW 2067, Australia

218 Lake Road
Northcote, Auckland, New Zealand

ISBN: 978 1 84537 262 0

Publishing Director: Charlotte Parry-Crooke
Commissioning Editor: Tim Jollands
Additional text: Ian Kearey
Editor: Ann Baggaley
Editorial Assistant: Rowena Curtis
Designer: Alan Marshall
Cartography: Julian Baker
Index: Janet Dudley

Reproduction by HBM Print Pte, Singapore
Printed and bound in Singapore by Tien Wah
Press Pte Ltd

FRONT COVER: The magnificent Hawa Mahal, the
'Palace of the Winds' in Jaipur.
SPINE: The Taj Mahal, Agra.
HALF TITLE: Farmer in wedding clothes, Ranakpur.
FRONTISPIECE: The Taj Mahal, Agra.
TITLE PAGE: *Namaste*

ACKNOWLEDGEMENTS

The author, principal photographer and publishers
would particularly like to express their gratitude
to the following for their generous and valuable
assistance during the preparation of this book:

Mark Tully • Adil Tyabji • Bikram Grewal • Toby
Sinclair • Rajgopal Nidamboor • Norma and
Maurice Joseph • Sue Thompson • Ian Kearey •
Charlotte Fox • Joe Hedges • Emily Hedges •
Taj Group of Hotels, London and Bombay • India
Book Distributors (Bombay) Ltd • India Government
Tourist Office, London • High Commission for
India, London • D.D.F.E. Resources

PLACE NAMES IN INDIA

Some of the names of places in India have recently, or over recent years, been changed back to their original Indian names. The following list gives the previous and current names of the main places affected. Alternative names for some places are also included. For ease of use, the generally more familiar, previous names are, for the most part, used in this book.

PREVIOUS NAME	CURRENT NAME	PREVIOUS NAME	CURRENT NAME	PREVIOUS NAME	CURRENT NAME
Alleppey	Alappuzha	Cochin	Kochi	Palghat	Palakkat/Palakaad
Baroda	Vadodara	Conjeevaram	Kanchipuram	Plassey	Palashi
Benares/Banaras/Benaras	Varanasi	Coondapoor	Kundapura	Panjim	Panaji
Bhuvaneshvar	Bhubaneshwar/	Coorg	Kodagu	Pondicherry	Puduchcheri
	Bhubaneswar	Courtallam	Kuttralam	Poona	Pune/Puné
Bombay	Mumbai	Ganges River	Ganga	Quilon	Kollam
Brindavan	Vrindavan	Gauhati	Guwahati	Ramnad	Ramanathapuram
Broach	Bharuch	Harmal	Arambol	Simla	Shimla
Calicut	Kozhikode	Hardwar	Haridwar	Sultan's Battery	Suthanbatheri
Cannanore	Kannur	Jamuna River	Yamuna River	Tanjore	Thanjavur
Cape Cormorin	Kanya Kumari/	Kutch	Kuchchh/Kachcha/Kachchh	Tellicherry	Thalasseri
	Kanyakumari/Kanniyakumari	Mercara	Madikeri	Tranquebar	Tharangambadi
Cauvery River	Kaveri River	Nagore	Nagur	Trichur	Thrissur
Cawnpore	Kanpur	Ootacamund/Ooty	Udagamandalam/	Trichy/Tiruchi	Trichchirappalli/
Changanacherry	Changanassery		Udhagamandalam		Tiruchirapalli
Cocanada	Kakinada	Palayankottai	Tirunelveli	Trivandrum	Thiruvanathapuram

CONTENTS

PREFACE

India profoundly altered my whole outlook on life, and in thirty years of living there I can't remember one of the countless visitors or longer-stay foreigners I have met, who has not been deeply moved by the country. Some of course have been shocked by the poverty, but most have found something in India they haven't found anywhere else in the world. They have delighted in its natural beauty, from the mighty Himalayas in the North, to the high hills and sun-drenched beaches of Kerala in the South. They have admired the great Hindu temples, and the Muslim monuments. But they have also sensed that India's ancient civilization stands for beliefs and values which are quite different from their own. India has always taught that man is part of nature, not nature's ruler, that God is revealed through myths not through historical events, and that all of us should seek to live balanced lives, not strive excessively for wealth, power or fame.

Indian civilization has survived centuries of alien rule – first Muslim and then British Christian – but it now faces the greatest of all the threats in its long history. It's the threat of a culture made powerful by its economic might, its apparent success and its control over the global media which, through satellite television, has the potential to penetrate the remotest Indian village. It's a culture which teaches exactly the opposite of India's traditional wisdom. It's based on the principle that nature is ours to investigate and exploit as we will. It teaches us that the goals of life are wealth and possessions. It puts the individual above the family, the community and society. It has no place for God or for myth.

I know of no one who is better able to bridge these two cultures than Shobita Punja — she has a deep understanding of modern Western culture, but her heart is Indian. This book is based on knowledge gained by years of meticulous research into India's past. But its author is no dry academic, because her writing is illuminated by a deep love and understanding of Indian mythology and philosophy.

Mark Tully
Delhi

PROFILE OF INDIA

The sprawling continent of Asia is as vast as it is varied. The earliest human civilizations flourished here, and new nations continue to be born. India, as defined by its present political boundaries, is a young Asian country. Currently it is the seventh largest country in the world. India's ancient culture has contributed a major chapter to the story of human development. It was not by conquest and exploitation that India earned a name but through her art, ideas, philosophy and idealism, the Taj Mahal and the non-violent message of Mahatma Gandhi, and it is these that will be remembered when the saga of human life on earth is being retold.

Variety and diversity are the keynotes of all that is Indian. This is amply reflected by the landscape. To the north, the earth's ancient landmass crushed continental plates to create the world's youngest and highest mountain system. The deserts of western India, inhabited by people dressed in resplendent hues, are balanced by the wetlands of the east, with their profusion of forests and trees. The chequered landscape of beautiful beaches and emerald islands, snow and desert dunes, forests and pasture land has given rise to rich, unique and diverse cultural experimentation. Each region of India has its own language, music, dance, architecture, painting, costume and food, with gods or goddesses to suit every human need and mood. The antiquity of the land is reaffirmed only by the continuity of Indian culture: the bullock cart designed 5,000 years ago wends its way even as jet planes fly overhead polluting the atmosphere.

THE LAND

India's physical features and geographical character have served both to segregate her from and integrate her with other world cultures. The north is bounded by the gigantic Himalayan mountain system that still safeguards Indian territory, while the famous passes of Jelep La and Nathu La on the Tibet–India route and the western Khyber pass on the Central Asia–Pakistan road provided restricted gateways into the subcontinent for travellers, traders and conquerors through the centuries.

The Himalayas, the abode (*laya*) of snow (*hima*), comprise three, almost parallel, ranges. This mountain wall, stretching for about 2,400 kilometres (1,500 miles) from Kashmir to Assam is in places 320 kilometres (200 miles) wide. Among the middle Himalayan range are peaks such as Nanda Devi and Annapurna that soar to heights of over 8,000 metres (26,000 feet). In 1953 Colonel John Hunt led the first expedition to Mount Everest (in the neighbouring country of Nepal) to successfully put human beings on the highest peak in the world (8,848 metres/29,029 feet). Subsequent expeditions have carried forward the colossal task of mapping this inhospitable region.

This mountain system within India, which stands like a curtain above the country, is divided into two geographical sections. The western Himalayan region extends from Kashmir to Kumaon and the eastern region extends from Sikkim and slopes gently to form the hills of Assam and the north-eastern states. Lush bamboo forests cover the foothills while the temperate zones are cloaked with rhododendron, sal, oak, maple and birch.

There are beautiful valleys in the western Himalayan region, notably Srinagar in Kashmir and Kulu in Himachal Pradesh. Hillsides clothed with forests and wild flowers, with waterfalls, clear mountain streams and lakes, complete the mountainscape. The valleys and foothills are verdant with evergreens, and on the loftier slopes one sees the graceful deodar, silver fir, juniper and shimmering flashes of the silver birch.

The Himalayas play a prominent role in Hindu mythology, for it is here, in the pristine snow, that the gods are said to live. From this sacred abode, embodying all that is spiritual and pure, flow the three largest river systems of the Indian subcontinent: the Indus to the west, the holy Ganga in the middle flowing west to east, and the Brahmaputra to the east. These rivers are largely snow-fed and flow perennially. From June to September the Himalayas act as a rain-break and block the south-westerly monsoon clouds. Heavy rainfall in these mountains causes the rivers to overflow and the plains below are often flooded with water carrying rich alluvium soil.

The basins of the Indus, the Ganga and the Brahmaputra form one of the world's largest expanses of flat alluvial plains, 2,400 kilometres (1,500 miles) in length and 320 kilometres (200 miles) across at the widest point. It was in these rich fertile river basins that the most ancient civilizations of the subcontinent first rose and flourished. Today the plains of

Above: *India's landscape is one of contrasts: in the Himalayan foothills a delicate tracery of snow highlights the winter landscape.*

PREVIOUS PAGES
Page 10: India is full of spectacle, colour and festival. In New Delhi, the President's Bodyguard stand in dignity along Vijay Chowk.
Page 11: In Varanasi, Uttar Pradesh, glorious silk brocade fabrics are made and sold.

the Ganga and Indus constitute the most densely populated areas on earth.

It was the river Indus that gave India her name, an anglicized version of Hindusthan, 'the land of the Indus'. In the 3rd century BC the armies of Alexander the Great of Macedonia and later, in the 10th century AD, the Muslim conquerors, crossed this river to enter Hindusthan. It is one of the ironies of history that today a major portion of the Indus flows through neighbouring countries like Pakistan, not through Indian territory.

The Ganga is unquestionably regarded as the most sacred of all rivers in India. It acquires its sanctity because it flows from the land of the gods, fertilizing the great plains below. It is to this river that the ashes of the dead are dedicated to ensure their return to divinity and immortality.

The western desert regions of India, Kuchchh and western Rajasthan, are poorly irrigated and neither the Ganga nor the Indus flow through this area. This arid region is divided into two: the Great Thar and the Little Thar deserts. Glimmering sand dunes and rocky limestone ridges characterize the landscape. Within the north-western area of the Little Thar are the ancient desert kingdoms of Jaisalmer and Jodhpur astride rocky plateaux overlooking a sea of sand.

The antithesis of the deserts of the west is to be found in eastern India where the Ganga and Brahmaputra rivers meet the Bay of Bengal, forming an enormous marshy delta. Here, exuberant mangrove forests abound with animal and insect life and exotic plants that thrive in the moist, humid climate.

The Himalayas in the north followed by the great Gangetic plains below are separated from the triangular Deccan peninsula in the south by a series of hill ranges, prominent among which are the ancient Aravalli, Vindhya and Satpura. These ranges are far older than the Himalayas and are therefore not as high, varying from 400 to 1,200 metres (1,300 to 4,000 feet). This hilly area and the rivers, such as the Narmada, which drain it also have a deep religious significance for the southern region, which, partitioned from the Gangetic valley, has

Sand dunes and scrub make up the Desert National Park: more than half of Rajasthan is desert or semi-arid land.

Stands of palm trees typify the tropical coastline of India's southern states, especially Kerala.

developed its own unique natural and cultural heritage. Up both sides of the peninsula runs a narrow coastal strip where the beaches are lapped by the Arabian Sea on the west and the Bay of Bengal on the east. Rising above the coastal strip are the Ghats, a range of low hills that form a wall around the central Deccan plateau. The Western Ghats are higher than their eastern counterparts and rise to heights of 460 to 1,220 metres (1,500 to 4,000 feet). The Eastern and Western Ghats culminate at the southern tip of the peninsula and form the lovely Nilgiri Hills or Blue Mountains.

Several sacred rivers replenish the fertility of peninsular India. The great Godavari flows from west to east and has the second largest river basin in the country, covering over 10 per cent of India's land area. The Krishna and the Kaveri, and other smaller river systems, water the southern states.

The Deccan plateau is considered the oldest part of the subcontinent, with geological strata several hundred million years old. Coal, diamonds and gold are found in this region. India was the only country in the ancient world to mine diamonds until they were discovered in Brazil and South Africa in 1725.

The Arabian Sea on the west coast brought traders and travellers from the Middle East and the coast of Africa to Indian shores for more than 2,000 years. The Bay of Bengal on the east coast enabled ancient communities from India to explore and establish trade contacts with Myanmar (Burma), Indonesia, China and Japan.

The Bay of Bengal and the Arabian Sea merge and mingle with the Indian Ocean. Dotting the deep blue waters are the tropical islands of Lakshadweep in the Arabian Sea and the Andamans (with over 201 islets) and Nicobar Islands in the Bay of Bengal. These islands form part of Indian territory, although the Andamans are a mere 311 kilometres (193 miles) from Cape Negris in Myanmar (Burma) and 1,190 kilometres (740 miles) from Chennai, the nearest Indian city.

CLIMATE

With geographical diversity comes a variety of climatic conditions in different parts of the country. There is snow in the Himalayan region, above 5,500 metres (18,000 feet). In the southern city of Chennai, temperatures range between 20° to 40°C (70° to 100°F), from hot, to hotter, to hottest.

Broadly speaking, India is said to have a tropical monsoon type of climate. In the northern and central regions there are four seasons. Winter lasts between November and March when it is cool and pleasant to travel, even in the desert regions of Rajasthan, and the brief springtime which follows brings blossoms and wild flowers to the foothills of the Himalayas.

The hot weather is ushered in by Holi, a popular north Indian festival, celebrated by children and adults alike playfully drenching each other with coloured water and powders in symbolic imitation of the hues of summer. During the season of Holi the flowering trees of the plains are a riot of colour: the orange-red of Gulmohur and Flame of the Forest, the pink blossoms of the Bauhinia, the delicate blooms of Persian Lilac and Jacaranda, the butter yellow bunches of the Indian Laburnum and showy flowers of Oleander. The profusion of colours is matched by the fragrance of the Jasmine and Pagoda trees.

As the heat builds up in northern India the earth blazes under a sky white with heat. Low pressures form in the northern plains that pull in the mighty monsoon winds from across the Indian Ocean and the Arabian Sea. The rains that fall between June and September are termed the south-western monsoon, for this is the route that they take. In May, dark clouds gather over the southern tip of India, and bring early rains and much needed respite to these tropical lands. The west coast of India assumes a spectacular aspect, with enormous grey clouds thundering over the sea, and it rains endlessly.

Then the monsoon clouds are drawn east-

Elephants are free to live natural lives in the wild in some of India's many parks and sanctuaries, such as the Corbett National Park in Uttaranchal.

WILDLIFE

With climatic conditions that range from arctic to tropical, India's wildlife is both rich and varied. Among the recorded species of Indian fauna there are over 40,000 different insects, 372 types of mammals, 1,228 species of birds and several hundred types of reptiles and fish. India can be divided into eight ecological zones—the western Himalayas, the eastern Himalayas, Assam, the desert, the Gangetic plain, the Deccan, the Malabar Coast in the south-west and the Andaman Islands—each of which has its own distinct species of plant, animal and bird life.

With the onslaught of 'development', many delicate ecological systems are being derailed by the effects of deforestation and the introduction of monoculture farming, mining and forms of pollution. While the poor, especially in rural areas, have an instinctive ecological understanding, insatiable consumerism in rich urban areas can lead to thoughtless plunder of India's natural heritage.

The most endangered species are the majestic Asian Elephant, the Greater One-horned Rhinoceros and, in the cat family, the regal Asiatic Lion, the Tiger and the Snow Leopard. There are several bird species, such as the Great Indian Bustard, Whitewinged Wood Duck, Blacknecked Crane and the Great Indian Hornbill, that also face extinction with the destruction of their natural habitat. Thousands of migratory birds from Siberia and Europe seek sanctuary in India during the fierce winter months and, with environmental change, cranes, pelicans and many other species are finding it increasingly difficult to locate undisturbed resting places.

In a valiant attempt to protect India's diverse wildlife, the government has initiated several programmes and projects, including the Central Ganga Authority to oversee the cleansing of the river, and the National Conservation Strategy to protect biosphere reserves such as the wetlands and coral reefs. Apart from government-funded projects, an encouraging number of non-government organizations are now working towards environmental conservation. The central government has established a network of national parks and sanctuaries covering a microscopic 4.5 per cent of India's total geographical area, and provides financial and technical assistance for their maintenance. A brief description of 10

ward by the low pressures in this region, providing Bengal and the eastern states with their quota of rain. Here the monsoon clouds hit the eastern Himalayan mountain barrier and swerve westward, drawn by the heat of the plains. By the time the entire expanse of southern and central India receives the monsoon rains it is already late in July–August. After the rains have watered the rest of the subcontinent, the clouds move westward. When the monsoons reach the western state of Rajasthan they are already spent and some of these areas receive no rainfall at all.

India's protected areas, such as Bharatpur, give sanctuary to hundreds of species of birds, including the colourful Indian Roller.

This annual cycle of rain is crucial for the growth of crops and the replenishment of water systems in rural and urban India. The annual monsoon is celebrated with festivals, music and dance, for the rural economy depends solely on these rains. A bad monsoon can have disastrous consequences. Widespread destruction of the tree cover of the Himalayan foothills, that plays such a critical role in regulating the monsoon rains and maintaining the ground water table, has caused floods, drought and misery in the northern and eastern states. Governments have collapsed as a consequence of the failure of the rains and the promise of a good harvest that the monsoon brings.

After the monsoons, the plains become hot and steamy once more. Then, between the months of October and November, comes the festival of lights, or Divali, heralding the short days and long dark nights of the winter months. A winter monsoon arrives from the north-east, across east Asia, over the Bay of Bengal. These winds blow across the southern-most states of India, Kerala, Tamil Nadu and Karnataka, without really affecting the northern parts of India. The gift of a second monsoon in winter nurtures the tropical jungles of Kerala and the lush vegetation of these areas, making them greener than any other part of the sub-continent.

representative sanctuaries and parks in principal ecological zones will give an idea of the wealth of Indian wildlife.

Corbett National Park was named after Jim Corbett, animal lover and the hunter of man-eating tigers. Following his advice, the park was established in 1936. It lies in the Sivalik foothills of the Himalayas, in the new state of Uttaranchal. The park offers wonderful opportunities for the study of animal, bird and plant life. The Ramganga river flows through it and the Mugger Crocodile and the Gharial, a fish-eating crocodile, are found both in its pools and on its rocky banks.

Around the river and the surrounding grasslands, the uneven hilly terrain is covered with sal and other varieties of native trees. This forested area is the home of over 50 species of animals, including the elusive Leopard and the Tiger. Indeed, Corbett National Park was one of the first game reserves to be associated with Project Tiger, the government-run campaign which provides special protection to this remarkable species, and it is estimated that about 30 to 35 tigers still inhabit it. Corbett is also the home of the Sloth Bear and the Himalayan Black Bear. Among the most rewarding sights are graceful Spotted Deer and Wild Boar roaming the forest, but the main attraction is the magnificent spectacle of majestic elephants living graciously in their natural environment.

The park offers organized elephant rides to visitors, enabling them to roam the jungle and observe wildlife. The best time to visit is between November and March. Corbett Park, and many others like it, are closed during the monsoons from the middle of June to November to allow the animals to remain undisturbed during the breeding season, and for the forest to recover from visitors.

Kaziranga National Park is an excellent example of the terrain and unique wildlife of eastern India. The park lies beside the mighty Brahmaputra river in the state of Assam. The river and the tropical wet climate preserve the rich moisture and lushness of the forest, enabling the largest population of One-horned Rhinoceros to live here. Not to be found in other states in India, this great creature is one of several endangered species, for it is hunted down by poachers who supply the horn to the tourist industry and, far worse, to meet the demands for aphrodisiacs in the Far East. The swamplands of Kaziranga are also the home of the Wild Buffalo, a creature with magnificent horns and a massive, dark body.

Great herds of Asian Elephants, 50 to 100 strong, pass through the forest, resting at the water-holes and beside the river. For the bird-lover, Assam and the eastern states of India provide exceptional opportunities to watch rare species in their natural habitat. To see the Bengal Florican fluttering and prancing amidst the tall grasses, the elegant eagles that soar above and colourful waterfowl are some of the greatest pleasures this park provides.

Manas National Park, also in the state of Assam, is unique for a multitude of reasons. Separated from the little kingdom of Bhutan by the Manas river, its landscape is amongst the most beautiful in India with the river meandering by pebble beaches, sandy banks and the lush jungle slopes of the Bhutan hills. This single park is home to over 19 of India's most endangered species. Here herds of elephants can be seen on their international expeditions to Bhutan for breakfast, and returning home to India for their evening bath. There are rhinos, Wild Buffalo, Gaur (the largest ox in the world), Swamp Deer, tigers and Pigmy Hogs. Often heard, but not seen, are several species of monkeys, including a rare group of Golden Langurs.

In spring, between March and April, when the flowering trees are in bloom, it is not unusual to see flocks of the most colourful birds in the world hovering and feeding in the trees. Scarlet minivets, dazzling bee-eaters, sunbirds and noisy bulbuls are omnipresent in this veritable garden of paradise.

Keoladeo Ghana National Park, Bharatpur, on the northern plains, 176 kilometres (110 miles) from Delhi in the state of Rajasthan, is unquestionably the best and most accessible bird sanctuary in India. Lying 370 metres (1,200 feet) above sea level, it comprises a number of lakes, wet marshy lands, scrub and wooded areas. There are well-marked paths for walking and bicycling, and boat rides may be taken through select regions. While three-quarters of the birds here are residents, over one-third migrate each year from Siberia, Central Asia and Europe. Several species breed and nest in Bharatpur, chiefly the Painted Stork, White Ibis, egrets and herons. A boat trip in the winter months into the secluded areas of the park provides a close look at the White Ibis, spoonbills, cormorants, the Bronze-winged Jacana, the Purple Moorhen and other water birds.

In late October, the migratory birds begin to arrive. The V-shaped flight formations of the Greylag and the Barheaded Geese are accompanied by flocks of ducks: Gadwall, Wigeon,

Today, the Tiger population of India is somewhere between two and three thousand. The White Tiger is a rare mutant.

Shoveler, Common Teal and Pochard. Rosy and Dalmatian Pelicans occasionally visit Bharatpur *en masse*, and at times it is hard to see the water for the birds.

Apart from the birds, and living companionably alongside their feathered friends, are the Wild Boar, the Sambar, India's largest deer, and the elegant Nilgai, or Blue Antelope. Rarely seen but active in these parts are the little Jungle Cat and the Fishing Cat. There are several points in the Bharatpur park where it is possible to see enormous pythons when they emerge from their burrows to sun themselves.

Ranthambore National Park, like Bharatpur, is in the state of Rajasthan. The landscape here is very different and the arid hills are the meeting place of the ancient Aravalli with the Vindhyan range. An enormous historical fort stands above looking down on the forest. The park, established in 1955, was one of the first areas to come under Project Tiger and is often in the news as tiger-lovers monitor the success of the programme. Research has shown that tigers, nocturnal hunters, have changed their habits and now roam the jungle of Ranthambore in broad daylight.

Tigers share the park with the Leopard, the second largest predator in the jungle. There are hyenas, jackals and smaller members of the cat family like the Jungle Cat. In the marshy lands of the lake, Marsh Crocodiles bask in the sun beside the waters.

Sambar, Chital or Spotted Deer and the Nilgai are commonly seen in the park. They are now quite used to tourists but keep their senses alert for predators. The park, with its lakes, water-holes and quiet forests, is also the home of several species of birds. The Crested Serpent Eagle in quest of small rodents and snakes, partridge and quail, and several types of stork can be spotted quite easily beside the waters.

Bandhavgarh National Park is one of the most exemplary wildlife reserves of central India. The park consists of grasslands, wooded areas, dense bamboo groves and rocky hill plateaux. In the centre is a huge, rugged flat-topped hill sporting a magnificent ancient fort. Along the footpath up to the fort and within its walls are ruins of medieval temples and massive stone sculptures. Some caves with inscriptions confirm that this area was inhabited 2,000 years ago.

The park is famous for its Tiger population, as indeed it should be. But there is a lot else to be seen. The Nilgai, Chausingha or Four-horned Antelope and Sambar are all to be found in the grasslands and forest areas. Wild Boar are common, while herds of Gaur (oxen) can be seen in the springtime moving down from the hills toward greener pastures. Recently the lively Chinkara (the Indian gazelle) was re-introduced into the park and it is a wonderful sight to see these delicate animals prancing in the grasslands. Exotic birds are on view, especially during the winter months. Most beautiful among them are the

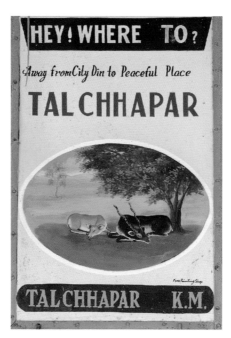

The display sign at Tal Chhapar Sanctuary in Rajasthan offers peace and quiet, as well as the possibility of viewing wildlife.

Malabar Hornbill, varieties of bee-eaters, parakeets, flycatchers and minivets.

Gir National Park and Lion Sanctuary was established in 1965 in the western state of Gujarat. This is the only place in the world, apart from city zoos, where one is likely to see the Asiatic Lion. The handsome male is smaller than his African cousin, and has a less flamboyant mane. Once the lion roamed freely in the jungles of northern and central India. Over the past few hundred years, during the Raj or colonial times and subsequently, this gracious creature has been entirely eradicated throughout the Asian continent and

today only the small population protected in the Gir sanctuary remains.

The Gir forest is dry for most of the year with scrub trees, like the Babul, and a few flowering trees. The park organizes trips at dawn and dusk through the jungle to enable visitors to see the lions on the prowl. They live in small prides and if one is very lucky one may see a lioness with her cubs. The forest also has Leopard, and Sambar, Chital or Spotted Deer, Nilgai, Chinkara and the usual community of Wild Boar and langur.

Pirotan Marine National Park and Sanctuary is also in the state of Gujarat. This, and some of the more restricted sanctuaries of the Andaman and Nicobar Islands, like those in Middle Button Island, Barren Island, North Reef Island and South Sentinel Island, are important preserves of Indian marine life.

The sanctuary and national park in Pirotan was established as late as 1980 and covers an area of over 457 square kilometres (176 square miles). Apart from a number of species of fish and other marine organisms, the park is famous for its turtle community. The Leather-backed and Olive Ridley turtles are among the fascinating species to be seen, and all the turtles here are on India's list of endangered species.

Just north of Gujarat is the Thar desert area of Rajasthan where a very different form of wildlife can be seen. The **Desert National Park** near Jaisalmer offers a unique opportunity to study this distinct environment and its inhabitants, which include Desert Wolf, fox, hare and Caracal.

Madumalai National Park in Tamil Nadu is an excellent example of the splendid forests and natural wealth of south India. It is connected to two other sanctuaries, the Wynad Sanctuary of Kerala and the Bandipur Tiger Reserve in Karnataka.

Established in 1938, Madumalai is watered by the Moyar river. Animal-watching on elephant back is one of the many pleasures that visitors can enjoy. Wild elephants also visit Madumalai and the adjoining sanctuaries. The main predators are the Tiger and Leopard which hunt Chital, Sambar, the tiny Barking Deer and the even smaller Mouse Deer which live in these lush forests. Running along the tree branches are the elusive Giant Squirrel and the rare Flying Squirrel.

The most colourful inhabitants of the forest are always the birds. Here, if one is lucky, one can see the giant Malabar Grey Hornbill, the Malabar Great Black Woodpecker and the Malabar Trogan. Barbets, parakeets and bee-eaters are more common in the area.

PEOPLE

India is home to just over a billion people. In 1901 the population was around 240 million. When India attained Independence, it was more than 320 million. Today, more than 25 per cent of India's population is below the age of 15, and in a few years these children will be adults with children of their own. Despite high birth-rates, large-scale population control programmes have been initiated by the government and voluntary agencies. Most poor families that earn less than a dollar a day often have more than three children. The older ones support the family by looking after their siblings, carrying water, collecting wood and assisting in farm work. Until related economic, social and educational challenges are addressed, little will be achieved in maintaining the balance of resources and population. However, the 2001 census report confirmed that literacy levels have risen substantially, and have even doubled in some areas.

Within this nation, the largest democracy in the world, there are various racial groups, religions and cultural backgrounds. There are more than four racial groups that have mingled, intermarried and lived together as a community for several thousand years. The Europoid peoples, descendants of Indo–Aryan communities, entered the Indian subcontinent nearly 3,500 years ago, settling in the Gangetic valley. Their literature refers to the dark-skinned native Dravidians who already inhabited the land. These two racial types blended together over centuries and at different historical periods the genetic proportions were reinforced. This is why in south India, the so-called heartland of Dravidian country, there are communities on the west coast with perfect brown complexions, blue-green eyes and naturally wavy hair. Similarly, Mongoloid features appear in varying degrees of intensity in the eastern states of Mizoram, Meghalaya, Nagaland, Manipur, Assam, and among the tribes of Orissa and Bihar. Here there are communities that look more like their Burmese neighbours than Indians from other

Holi, the festival of colours or the festival of spring, is one of the most eye-catching events in a land of spectacle and ritual. In early March, mostly throughout northern India, soaking and getting soaked with coloured water and powder heralds the summer.

states. In the far-flung Andaman Islands there are some purer strains of the Negroid race.

India is not evenly populated. In the Gangetic plain, Uttar Pradesh is India's most populous state, and has over 16.44 per cent of the country's inhabitants. The population of the north-eastern Himalayan state of Sikkim has only .05 per cent of the Indian total, or approximately 540,000 people, while the city of Mumbai has an estimated population of 13 million. The population density also varies from region to region: the capital city of Delhi

India has a rich diversity of peoples and dress. In the north, woollen clothes and scarves are commonly worn (top left); *for Sikhs* (bottom left) *uncut hair* (kesh), *worn under a turban, is central to their religion; frilled turbans – and splendid moustaches – are often part of an official uniform* (top right), *while decorative veils adorn the women of Rajasthan* (bottom right).

has an average of over 7,000 people living in an area of one square kilometre (²/₅ square mile) while the state of Arunachal Pradesh is sparsely populated, with merely 10 people per square kilometre.

To complicate matters, there is the floating population of thousands of migrants that moves from rural areas to the cities every day of the year in pursuit of a livelihood. India has also given political asylum to millions of refugees. In the wake of the fall of Tibet to the Chinese, the Dalai Lama brought his followers to India in 1953. Today, there are Tibetan schools, institutions and hospitals for Tibetan people living in India. Similarly, when Bangladesh became an independent country

separate from Pakistan, thousands of refugees were displaced during the war and were rehabilitated on Indian soil. Then there are cross-cultural syntheses, such as that of the small, but significant, population of Anglo-Indians. This community has its own distinct cultural identity and strong opinions about what 'home' means. Many Anglo-Indians are the offspring of marriages or liaisons between British colonial officers or other ranks with the native population. They dress in western clothes, are baptized with Christian names, but are Indian.

LANGUAGES

The multitude of languages spoken in India provides some indication of the complexity of

Indian society. There are over 1,652 different dialects, many of which are derived from four main sources. Sanskrit, like Latin, an ancient classical language that is now no longer spoken, is the basis of several north Indian languages as diverse as Hindi, Bengali and Gujarati. The Dravidian family of languages has four ancient branches from which stem Tamil (spoken in Tamil Nadu), Telugu (now spoken in Andhra Pradesh), Kannada (of Karnataka) and Malayalam (of Kerala). The tribal dialects of Orissa and Bihar do not belong to any of these root languages. There are also popular hybrids such as the poetic Urdu language which has its roots in the intermingling of Hindi and Persian in the army camps of the medieval period and is spoken in northern India, Bihar and the Deccan.

The government has recognized 16 major Indian languages that are taught in schools, and in which legal and official transactions can take place. All these languages are sufficiently advanced to serve as the medium of instruction at university level. Each has its own literary heritage, ancient texts, religious works, classical drama and poetry. Today, most regional languages have separate newspapers and a film industry of their own.

After Independence, India was divided into a federation of states formed on the basis of linguistic criteria. Some believe this has been the cause of much social unrest and created unnecessary barriers to the formation of a unified India. Today, there is no state where people speak just one language or dialect. In fact, India is more like Europe, where many people speak more than one language and schools generally follow a three-language formula. For historical reasons, dating back to the colonial period, English tends to be the language of the elite, of those privileged enough to go to school and college. Knowledge of English is still a ticket to jobs and upward mobility in

Whether working (in Madhya Pradesh; top right) or relaxing (in Jaipur; bottom right), the women of India combine elegance and colour. Sadhus, holy men (bottom left), often semi-naked and with their skins smeared with ash, are seen wandering throughout India.

India, as it is in most of Asia. As a measure of its authority, there are over 50 English news-papers for the relatively small percentage who speak and read this language.

If language indicates the complexity of a culture, India is a perfect model. With language diversity comes the multiplicity of beliefs, food habits, costumes and customs. In Tamil Nadu, a Muslim and a Hindu may share a mother tongue, but their religion can be easily distinguished—Tamil spoken by a Brahmin is different from that spoken by a member of any other community.

HINDUS

More than 82 per cent of the population of the country are designated 'Hindu' or 'Dalits'. 'Hindu' is a term derived from the word 'Indus' and once referred to those who lived in Hindusthan, the land beyond the river, but has now come to mean a way of life and a religion.

Hindus have no single supreme leader or messiah, nor do they have a single religious text like the Bible or *Koran* to which they adhere. The Hindu philosophy of life has evolved over many centuries, with each generation absorbing ideas from the tribal and rural practices with which it came into contact. The oldest known religious texts are the four *Vedas* that formed part of an enormous oral tradition which was committed to the written word only centuries later. The *Vedas* explain the rites and rituals due to the various gods and goddesses, most of whom personify natural elements. For example, the lord of the skies, thunder and lightning was Indra, and Agni was the lord of fire of both the hearth and the sacrificial altar. As agriculture and technology enabled human beings to gain greater control over nature and the elements, these older deities were superseded by other gods and goddesses.

Later the *Upanishads* and the *Bhagavad*

Gita of the *Mahabharata* epic offered a more abstract philosophical world view. Everything was created from the same source but manifested in varying forms. The supreme aim of life was to find that path which would break the cycle of life, death, distress, unfulfilled desires and strife and lead human beings to the original source, immortality and everlasting joy. Everyone has to find his or her path, so gurus and religious leaders could not dictate or prescribe the way, nor could much be achieved by conversion by the sword, or missionaries of the faith. The only aid to finding the most suitable path was wisdom. Great emphasis is placed in the Hindu tradition on wisdom, the light of knowledge that expels the darkness of ignorance. There is no concept of sin, good or bad, only degrees of wisdom. Those who have found peace are wise, those who are unhappy are still ignorant.

This philosophical tradition of finding one's own path to eternal life is reflected in the tolerance that Hinduism has shown to other religions and other paths. There were sages who were atheists, others offered their passionate worship to one god, yet others followed the path of yoga, controlling the body and mind to achieve great strengths, physical and mental, and there were those who worshipped their ancestors, or lived for the service of their fellow creatures. These many paths, forms of worship and beliefs were incorporated into the greater Hindu tradition and the way a Brahmin offers his prayers is quite different from how tribal worship is conducted. In essence they both honour the elements and the source of all creation, and their prayers are yearnings to return to that state of universal wisdom.

CASTE SYSTEM

Unfortunately, in the course of history and under the pressures of economics and property control, the path and chosen way came to be dictated by birth. The caste system became rigid and by the 6th century BC, the path for a child born in a priestly family was assigned by the family tradition. The Brahmins held the key to knowledge for the entire community, they wrote the sacred texts and performed rituals in the temple. The ruling (warrior) class or Kshatriyas were born to rule, their path clearly on the plane of physical action, warfare and the protection of others. Those born in the Vaishya community were by profession farmers and merchants, and it was in fulfilling their social and occupational duties that they would attain *moksha*, or salvation from the cycle of life. At the bottom of the social ladder was the vast sea of humanity who lived by serving the other three castes. This group, called Shudras, was not a homogenous community, and included those who had been subjugated in times of war, those who belonged to occupational groups, such as leatherworkers, and tribal peoples who worshipped their own distinct deities.

These four castes, based on occupations and economic security, had their prescribed place in the religious hierarchy and rules for performance of rituals. But the caste system was never static and the process of evolution or social segmentation continued for 3,000 years. *Jati* became the criteria that prescribed who one could marry and with whom one could eat. The *jati* system is so complicated that within the Brahmin caste a family of temple priests would not marry into a family of priests who conducted funerals. Similarly, a Shudra leatherworker would not marry into a family of blacksmiths. The *jati* of an individual soon prescribed the gods to be worshipped, the path of salvation to be

followed, social etiquette and religious customs, making it extremely complex to explain the concept of Hindu society. Within this system there are upper-caste vegetarian Brahmins of south India who will not eat root vegetables such as garlic or onions; equally there are Brahmin families in Bengal who eat fish. The social equation of religion became a question of birth and the family to which an individual belonged. Throughout the history of the evolution of the Hindu way of life there were sages, poets and philosophers who revolted against the socio-economic foundation that had corrupted their faith, questioning

A Hindu temple custodian dressed in similar attire to that of the sadhus, *the wandering holy men of India.*

the social supremacy of the Brahmins, emphasizing that the divine had no caste, and arguing that the path to enlightenment could not be dictated by caste, birth or family.

BUDDHISTS

Famous among these so-called 'protesting' sages was the Buddha who lived approximately 2,500 years ago. Gautam Siddhartha belonged to a Kshatriya ruling caste family, and was born in Lumbini in an area now in Nepal. Brought up to be king, he renounced his royal home when he was barely 25 years old and wandered through the Gangetic

plains, stopping at religious centres to discuss the meaning of life with philosophers and teachers. Unconvinced by the established norms of the times, he retired to Gaya in Bihar to meditate for 40 days and nights. Rather than accepting what birth and teachers prescribed, Siddhartha searched within himself for eternal knowledge. He is said to have attained enlightenment, the wisdom to comprehend the Universal Truth, and came to be called the Buddha. He then wished to pass the rest of his days in meditation, but was persuaded by a few disciples to teach them. The Buddha gave his first sermon in a place called Sarnath, outside the great Hindu pilgrimage centre of Varanasi.

The corpus of the Buddha's teachings has been compiled in a number of texts and explains the essence of his philosophy. The 'Four Noble Truths' proclaim that all life is sorrowful, that the cause of suffering is ignorant craving for material wealth and transient pleasure, that suffering can come to an end by following the eightfold path. This teaching struck at the heart of caste society, eliminating the need for a Brahmin as a mediator in rituals and advocating the native language rather than the Brahmin tongue as the medium of prayer. Wealthy mercantile families and other communities afforded no social mobility in the Hindu caste system became adherents of the way of the Buddha.

Buddhism as a way of life was adopted by several rulers of the Indian subcontinent. Large institutions and religious centres were established with this patronage. Several years after the Buddha's death two major branches of Buddhist thought emerged: one called *Hinayana*, the little vehicle, and the other *Mahayana*, the great vehicle that carries one to salvation.

From the Indian subcontinent the teachings of the Buddha spread to neighbouring Sri Lanka, the north-west frontier, Myanmar (Burma), Thailand, Indonesia, China, Korea and finally to Japan. In the 10th and 12th centuries, as Muslim armies began to conquer territories in India, several Buddhist institutions were destroyed. Idol worship, not permissible under Islam, came under threat and

Buddhist monks fled from mainland India to shelter in the Himalayan mountains. In time, these retreats, in the valleys of Tibet, Bhutan, Nepal and Ladakh in India, became famous centres of learning. Here, manuscripts, sciences and rituals and the gentle way of the Buddha were preserved over the centuries.

JAINS

Vardhamana Mahavir, also of royal Kshatriya descent, was a contemporary of the Buddha. He is considered the last of the 24 Tirthankaras (makers of the crossing over, or pathfinders) of the Jain religion. As in Buddhism, the philosophy of the Jains also questioned the authority of the Brahmins and the legitimacy of the caste system. In this philosophy the human soul is described as a crystal, pure and clean, which is stained and grows dark with every evil action and violent act. The darkened soul, registering violence and hatred, journeys from one life of pain to another, until it attains the wisdom to cleanse itself. *Ahimsa*, non-violence and peaceful coexistence with all living creatures, not merely other human beings, is the prescribed path to purity of soul and salvation.

Unlike the small Buddhist community, the Jains in India today comprise a population of three million. The philosophy of the Jains appealed to those communities that were denied privileges within the Hindu caste system. Even today, prominent bankers, diamond merchants, traders and moneylenders belong to the Jain community. With such wealthy patronage, beautiful Jain temples were built in several places in India. The Jain community, under its doctrine of service to others, has also set up numerous charitable organizations, hospitals and schools.

MUSLIMS

Muslims form the second largest majority in India, constituting 11.7 per cent of the population. The religion, comparatively young by Indian standards, was introduced into India first by Arab traders in the 7th century and later by Muslim rulers. The principal tenets of Islam were established by Prophet Muhammed. He was born in Mecca in AD 570

and earned his living in the harsh desert, tending camels. Arabia was then a tribal country stricken by internecine warfare. Idols and images were worshipped, and might of the sword was the law. At the age of 40 Muhammed received the divine gift of the word of God, Allah. Though unable to write himself, the humble prophet had these words recorded and this became the holy book, the *Koran*. On the basis of his teachings he was able to unite the warring tribes of Arabia, introduce monotheism and a universal system of law far in advance of the times.

Over the next few centuries, the Arab conquests spread Islam to the shores of the Atlantic and east to Persia. North-western

Muslims at the Jama Masjid in Old Delhi. One wears a silver locket containing a text from the Koran.

India was regularly raided and finally rulers conquered the vast plains of the north and made India their home. They built mosques for prayer and schools for study. In the 16th and 17th centuries Mughal emperors like Akbar, and his great-grandson, Dara Shikoh, encouraged the translation of Hindu texts such as the *Upanishads* and the epic poems, the *Ramayana* and *Mahabharat*, in order to comprehend the principles of Hindu philosophy. While Islam was a new religion of the ruling classes, the approach of the Sufis, the sect of mystic Islamic poets, was not dissimilar to the Hindu form of *bhakti* worship. In both the Sufi and *bhakti* tradition the mystic poets expressed great personal love for the divine and a universal love for humankind. Even

today festivals honouring the great poet-philosophers, Moin-ud-Din Chisti of Ajmer and Nizam-ud-Din Aulia of Delhi, draw active participation from both the Muslim and Hindu communities.

Beginning as it did as the religion of the rulers in medieval India, and at the same time appealing to the sentiments of the common man, Islam took root very quickly in Indian soil. When the British were obliged to free India from colonial rule, the demand for a separate Muslim country was raised and Pakistan was born. But Partition, and the division of a land that had shared a common heritage, caused enormous bloodshed and suffering. Families were broken up, friends separated and a great culture torn apart. Even today, the scars have not really healed.

SIKHS

Guru Nanak, the founder of one of the world's youngest religions, was greatly influenced by both Hindu and Muslim traditions. He was born in 1469, in a place that now lies in Pakistan. He was succeeded by ten gurus and their followers derived their name 'Sikh' from the Sanskrit word *shishya*, meaning student. The teachings of the gurus were compiled in the holy book called the *Guru Granth Sahib*, which is a symbol of the divine. The Sikh community honours one god, derived from Hindu philosophy, and worship no idol in the manner of the Muslims. They place a strong emphasis on a casteless society, following the Islamic belief that all men are equal in the eyes of God. In their *gurdwaras*, their place of prayer, rich, influential or poor are given equal status, eating in the community kitchen and praying together.

Hindus and Sikhs intermarry, have been closely related in customs, share in each other's festivals and worship freely in each other's temples. However, tension and strained relationships developed between the Sikhs and Islamic rulers of northern India during the Mughal period. With the torture and killing of the fifth Guru, Arjun Dev, the friction between the two groups vying for power heightened. The persecuted Sikh community forged a new identity, militant, powerful and easily identifiable, donning the saffron turban of sacrifice, and wearing the unshaven beard and long uncut hair.

Today the Sikhs form 2 per cent of the population, which is smaller than the Christian community in India. They live mainly in northern India, in the agriculturally wealthy state of Punjab. Their enterprising spirit has taken them to the far corners of the globe. Over the past decade militant groups within their community have been building up a case for an exclusive Sikh homeland but the Indian government (with not always the gentlest hand) has curbed the movement for the time being.

PARSIS

In the 8th century, when the Arabs conquered Persia, a small community of Persians migrated to India. They brought with them their ancient religion and customs. Zoroaster, founder of the religion, lived in the 6th century BC. His teachings are set out in the Zoroastrian holy scripture called *Zend-Avesta*. This religion places absolute faith in one god, Ahura Mazda, who is worshipped through the purest element on earth, fire. Zoroastrian temples were built wherever this community settled on Indian soil. The temple has no idol within, only the holy fire, which must be kept continuously burning by initiated priests.

The Parsis, meaning the Persians, adapted to Indian conditions. Most of them settled on the west coast, in the state of Gujarat and around Mumbai. They adopted the local language, Gujarati, and assumed also the local attire and food habits. This is an extremely small, though influential, community that chooses to marry only within its confines.

JEWS

A very small community of Jews live in India. For historical reasons they settled in Kochi (Cochin), in Kerala, and some Bene Israelis live in and around Mumbai. India has had trade relations with the Middle East for the past 2,000 years and possibly a small community of traders ventured to live on Indian soil over 1,000 years ago to establish links between the two regions. In Kochi the little Jewish quarter resembles a town in Israel, with cobbled streets, large warehouses for storing spices for export, and a local synagogue. The synagogue has in its collection engraved copperplates that establish that the Jewish community was granted land to settle and was sanctioned trading rights by the local ruler. Today a number of Jews from India have migrated to Israel and America. This has sadly depleted the Jewish population which so perfectly epitomizes the rich diversity of Indian people and their heritage.

CHRISTIANS

Historically, Christianity was introduced into India at two points in time. In south India, largely the west coast of Kerala, Christianity arrived with the early traders. Trade links with the Middle East had brought Phoenicians, Greeks, Jews, Christians and Arabs in search of commerce and wealth. It is also believed that St Thomas, one of Jesus Christ's twelve apostles, came to India to preach the new faith and died in the town of Chennai. A small but powerful community of Syrian Christians and other denominations, who are descendants of these early converts, follow the oldest form of Christian worship. In some ways their church service is similar to that of the ancient Greek Orthodox church.

With the establishment of colonial rule in the subcontinent in the last few hundred years, further conversions took place. In Goa and in south India the Catholic church still has a strong following. Part of British, French and Portuguese colonial policy was to nurture a native community in the etiquette of their home country so that they would assist the foreign rulers. Protestant and Catholic missionaries working in India and the north-eastern states set up schools, hospitals and charitable institutions. In Indian churches, hymns are sung, and the entire church service is conducted in the local language. By contrast, in prestigious Christian schools, English was taught as the first language and introduced generations of children nurtured on Christian values and western traditions.

During the British period many aspects of Hindu and Muslim society came under colonial scrutiny. Educated Indians, influenced by Christian traditions, sought to cleanse their culture of the evils of the caste system, widow burning and other superstitious customs.

With perhaps wider vision than anyone before him, Mahatma Gandhi furthered these efforts by striving to restore the dignity of the lower castes, to create an India where all religions could live and work together without fear. His assassination in 1948, just a year after Independence, was an indication of how difficult the task was.

HISTORY

The fascination of India lies in her ancient heritage which, unlike that of most other countries, continues to be a part of her contemporary culture. The continuity of traditions, age-old customs and artistic legacy alongside the modern world gives Indian life and society richness, colour and depth.

STONE AGE

India has been inhabited for millennia. Rich natural resources and favourable climate made it possible for human ancestors to live in this vast subcontinent. Thousands of centuries later, *Homo sapiens* settled in communities, developing the simple tools that distinguished modern man from his forefathers. The earliest remains of roughly carved stone flints and tools have been

Catholicism was introduced into Goa by the Portuguese in the early 16th century; colourful processions are a part of the many Christian festivals still celebrated during the year.

discovered in central and eastern India. There are several sites where these early dwellers lived. In Bhimbetka, in the state of Madhya Pradesh, there are a number of well-preserved natural caves, on the floors of which were found flintstones and carvings made by human beings over 8,000 years ago. The caves are located near forest areas and streams that provided the early inhabitants with their bare necessities. The cave walls bear the remains of prehistoric paintings.

INDUS VALLEY CIVILIZATION

With the evolution of stone tools, the domestication of animals and the planting of annual crops, significant changes occurred in the lifestyle of these early inhabitants. There are several sites in northern and central India that confirm that the Neolithic age saw the progression to a more settled way of life. The cultivation of crops beside a great river such as the Indus must have yielded great benefits. With the growth of villages came a prosperous economy and the inception of trade.

Evidence of a thriving agricultural economy came with a remarkable discovery early in this century. In the process of laying a railway track in the Punjab, the workers found great mounds of large bricks, and on further investigation a township called Harappa was excavated. In 1920, an Indian archaeologist, R.D. Banerjee, visited a site in Sind (now in Pakistan) which the villagers had nicknamed Mohenjodaro, the 'Mound of the Dead'. Four years later, John Marshall, director of the Archaeological Survey of India, while studying the excavations at Mohenjodaro, situated near the mouth of the Indus, realized that the artefacts found here were very similar to those discovered in Harappa, nearly 645 kilometres (400 miles) away. It was found that both the sites were over 5,000 years old and contemporary to Chinese, Mesopotamian and Egyptian cultures. Evidence from the Indus Valley Civilization, as it was called, was also found in ancient Mesopotamian sites, revealing that trade links had existed between these two historic civilizations. Subsequent excavations have unearthed over 400 Indus Valley sites as far east as the region around Delhi and as far south as Gujarat and Mumbai.

Each of the cities of the Indus Valley Civilization was built to a grand master plan organized on a grid system. Broad roads into the city met at right angles with smaller con-

Some of the earliest paintings and artefacts made in prehistoric times were found in the Bhimbetka caves in Madhya Pradesh.

necting roads and service lanes. Uniform blocks of buildings were erected along the main roads. The city had clearly identifiable residential areas, commercial sections and workshops. A prominent area with a citadel housing the great granary and bath was found in Mohenjodaro. The houses in all the cities were markedly similar, most of them two-storeyed, with a courtyard, bathing and cooking rooms, and living apartments. A sophisticated underground sewerage network carried waste to the nearest river.

The residential areas contained a vast collection of wheel-thrown pottery, painted clay household goods and semi-precious stone jewellery. The Indus Valley Civilization also marks the bronze age of Indian history. Bronze axes, agricultural and fishing tools and ornaments were excavated.

Most intriguing of all the finds were the seals. All the cities of the Indus Valley Civilization yielded a large collection of seals bearing images of human, animal and mythical creatures. The seals, often just a few centimetres long, also bore inscriptions, evidence of a very early script used by the citizens. The script has not yet been deciphered but, when it is, it will undoubtedly provide important

information on the people of these ancient metropolises.

IRON AGE

Archaeological evidence indicates that as the cities of the Indus Valley Civilization were being abandoned, the population moved towards the great Gangetic valley. During this period, as nomadic communities from West and Central Asia moved to the region of Persia, the Middle East and on to Europe, another group entered the plains of northern India. There is a common generic base to all the languages that evolved in the lands where these groups settled.

These nomadic pastoral people discovered lush forests and fertile lands. As they settled in their new territories they cut down the forests and established villages. Recent historical theories suggest that the indigenous population may have already acquired the agricultural skills necessary for the cultivation and habitation of the Gangetic valley during this period. Society was first structured on the basis of tribal laws, where male and female had more or less equal rights. With the development of agriculture and the possession of property, laws governing marriage and inheritance assumed a patrilinear pattern. The female goddesses and earth mother of the early tribal period were soon superseded by male deities.

The structure of society grew in complexity with the evolution of trade, skilled professions and crafts. Iron tools found at these habitations also suggest that agricultural practices were revolutionized. The increase in produce was an incentive to trade. By 1000 BC, India had become inhabited by small tribal republics and kingdoms that had begun to trade with communities near and far.

From Buddhist literature it is apparent that by about 500 BC a large portion of northern Indian society had become rigidly entrenched in the caste system and occupations were dictated by birth. In the Buddha's lifetime there were great pilgrimage centres and thriving cites like Varanasi that attracted both the skilled trader and also the philosopher. Kings inherited their thrones and were no longer chosen by the community on the basis of their performance or aptitude. Wealthy merchants and trading communities subscribed to the Buddhist faith and gave generously to the monasteries. There are inscriptions that record such gifts, and several large Buddhist centres were set up in north and central India. Buddhism also travelled further south to Tamil Nadu, and Jain centres were also established in Karnataka.

VISITORS FROM THE WEST

Contemporary literature from Persia, India and Greece suggests that this period was one of great development and activity. The republics and kingdoms of the Buddha and Mahavir were well established on sound administrative principles. By the 6th century BC the small but powerful kingdom of Magadha had been founded in the region of Pataliputra, modern day Patna in the eastern Indian state of Bihar. King Bimbisara of Magadha and his successors engaged in a series of battles and managed to secure a vast kingdom that spread over the eastern and central areas of the Gangetic valley.

During this time, the Achaemenid emperor of Persia crossed the mountain barriers of north-western India and added new territories to his already large empire. This contact with Persian civilization had considerable influence on both Indian and Persian cultures, and led to the establishment of trade contacts. Around 327 BC, Alexander the Great, having driven his army through the Middle East and finally defeated the Persian emperor, arrived in north-western India. Unable to persuade his homesick army to go any further, Alexander was forced to turn back. He died of malarial fever in 323 BC, on the homeward journey to Macedonia.

The conquest of the north-western region by Alexander had a far-reaching impact on the history and culture of India. Alexander left behind a number of able administrators to govern his empire. Seleucus Nikator, his general and successor, took charge of the territory and opened up trade links and networks that spread from the European continent through the Middle East, Persia and into India. The kingdom of Magadha offered the only resistance to the progressive spread of Greek control. Chandragupta inherited the throne in 320 BC and with his strong army was able to halt the spread of Greek colonies, incorporating the north-western region and the Punjab within his own kingdom. Chandragupta's son, Bindusara, continued his father's expansionist policy and left to his son, Ashok, a large, justly administered empire. The Mauryan empire, as it was now called, inherited by Ashok (c.270-

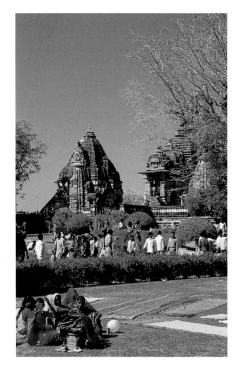

Built between AD 950 and 1050, the temples of Khajuraho were the creation of the Chandella dynasty, and represent central Indian architecture at its most magnificent.

232 BC) was further enlarged when he conquered the great region of Kalinga (in the modern states of Orissa and northern Andhra Pradesh).

After the death of Ashok, the enormous, unified Mauryan empire began to crumble. The Gandharan region was lost to Bactrian Greek rulers, who were in turn superseded by the Parthians. Then came hordes of militant rulers from Central Asia, most successful amongst them the Kushans, who eventually brought a large portion of north India under their rule. Trade flourished and the kings patronized the arts. The Kushans controlled the trade routes between India, Persia and the Roman empire in the west and lucrative commercial ventures with China in the east.

THE GUPTAS

When the Kushans were beginning to lose their grip over northern India, the power of another dynasty, the Gupta, was growing in eastern India. Chandragupta assumed the throne in the 4th century AD and his son Samudragupta established the capital of his kingdom at Pataliputra. In the south there

were other kingdoms, such as that of the Cholas, with whom the Guptas had cordial relations. It was during this period of relative peace that great ventures were undertaken in trade and commerce. Ships and trading communities explored the vast wealth of Myanmar (Burma), Indonesia, Cambodia and China. Excavations of Gupta sites have yielded such large quantities of gold coins that this period is often nicknamed the 'golden age'.

In the field of art and architecture, the Gupta period heralded new and monumental experiments. Great rock-cut caves and prayer halls were hewn out of the hillsides of Ajanta in Maharashtra, while simple stone structural temples were built in north and central India. Music, dance, literature and all the sciences practised were systematically documented during this period. It was the age of documentation and classification, and great manuscripts on grammar, astronomy, philosophy, medicine, even the *Kama Sutra*, the art and science of love-making, were compiled. There are literary references to great Sanskrit plays being staged for royal audiences. With the wealth brought by Indian and foreign trade a new community of patrons of the arts also came into being, and the texts and manuscripts of the time reflect a highly sophisticated and cultured society.

A long line of weak Gupta rulers saw the end of a politically large, unified north India. The end was catalyzed when the north was invaded by hordes of Huns under rulers with their base in Afghanistan who pushed gradually into the western region of Gujarat and Rajasthan. From the resulting turmoil came the forceful reign of Harsha who ascended the throne in AD 606 and ruled for over 40 years from his capital in Kanauj.

KINGDOMS OF THE SOUTH

Beyond the control of the Gupta empire rose smaller but equally influential kingdoms in the Deccan and southern India. In the region of Tamil Nadu, a powerful dynasty known as the Pallavas had their port towns and seaside centres in places like Mahabalipuram, outside the present-day city of Chennai. A thriving sea trade with Java and the Far East took Pallava culture to distant shores, where even today it can be seen in the temples of Prambanan in Java and *Ramayana* theatre performances of the Javanese islands.

By the end of the 9th century Pallava rule

was overshadowed by the rising power of the Chola kings, whose empire at its zenith stretched from the Gangetic plain to Sri Lanka, with trading posts in Java, Sumatra and China. Huge temples were constructed during this period under royal patronage in Thanjavur and adjoining cities. Crafts such as bronze casting, textile weaving and the creation of jewellery flourished, strengthening further the Chola economy.

STRUGGLES IN THE NORTH

After the death of Harsha in the middle of the 7th century there was a scramble for the throne. Two dynasties benefited the most — the Palas of eastern India in the regions of Bengal, Orissa and Bihar, and the Prathiharas of central and northern India. The rivalry between these two contenders did not prevent the construction of beautiful temples in their kingdoms and the establishment of individual regional cultures.

The Prathiharas leave the pages of Indian history exhausted by battles with neighbouring kings. The final blow came with the raids of Mahmud of Ghazni who overpowered them in the 11th century. The break up of the Prathihara kingdom provided an opportunity for a number of small principalities to seize political control over north and central India. Under this fragmented rule, despite the troubled, unsettled times, prosperous cities were built, old ones enlarged, and forts and magnificent temples constructed. The 10th century in western, central and eastern India was a period of affluence with a cultural exuberance comparable to that in the south.

INVASIONS FROM THE NORTH

In contrast to the raids of Mahmud of Ghazni, Muhammed Ghori, another Afghan chieftain, had established his rule in Sind and Lahore by 1182. He then set his sights on conquering the plains of northern India and adding the region to his growing kingdom. The Rajput clans ruling the western region of Rajasthan and Prithviraj Chauhan, the ruler of Delhi, were no match for Muhammed Ghori's well-

equipped army and the first Islamic sultanate was established with Delhi as its capital by 1193. The new ruler had the first stone mosque built on Indian soil in Delhi. Muhammed Ghori died in 1203 and was succeeded by his able commander and one-time slave, Qutub-ud-Din Aibek, who founded the Slave or Mamluk dynasty.

News of the wealth and prosperity of India spread through Persia and Afghanistan, and soon the Slave dynasty fell in battle to the Afghan Khaljis. Ala-ud-Din Khalji also established his capital in Delhi, built a new fort and added to Qutub-ud-Din's mosque.

In turn, Ala-ud-Din's vast empire was to fall into the hands of his appointed governor Ghiyas-ud-Din, heralding in the remarkable reign of the Tughluqs. Ghiyas-ud-Din Tughluq built a new capital fort in Delhi and in his short reign succeeded in establishing a secure position in the Indian subcontinent. The Tughluq dynasty was weakened by the struggle for

The Portuguese influence can be seen throughout Goa. The ruins of Fort Aguada, once an important stronghold, stand where the Mandovi river flows into the Arabian Sea.

power with smaller principalities and eventually succumbed to the Sayyid family, who had allied themselves with the great Mongol despot, Timur.

The Sayyids were soon displaced by the Afghan Lodis who also settled in Delhi, adorning the city with their tombs. Sikandar Lodi later moved the seat of power to Agra where a new fort and palaces were built.

THE PORTUGUESE

European efforts to capture Arab-dominated trade with the east were spearheaded in the subcontinent by the Portuguese. They established a settlement in Kochi in the state of Kerala, on the west coast of India. Pedro Alvarez Cabral, the Portuguese adventurer and explorer, brought with him Franciscan friars and set up a church in Kochi.

On his historic voyage in 1497, Vasco da Gama sailed from Portugal along the African coast, via the Cape of Good Hope, then across the Indian Ocean, landing on the west coast. He obtained permission to trade from the local ruler and by the time he left in 1502 he had established a fleet of ships to patrol the west coast, to ward off pirates and to protect Portuguese interests. In 1510, Vasco da Gama's commander captured Goa from the Sultan of Bijapur and established the Portugese eastern empire on Indian soil. New Portuguese townships, forts, palaces and churches were built in Goa. Portuguese trade contacts were replaced by colonial rule, with administrators introducing laws to govern the new colony. Goa was liberated from the Portuguese in 1961.

THE MUGHAL EMPIRE

Meanwhile the Lodi empire established itself in northern India. Conflict within the Lodi family led one branch to make an alliance with a descendant of Timur's family, Babur from Kabul. From Lahore, Babur went on to win a decisive battle at Panipat in 1526 that gave him entry into the Gangetic plain. Occupying Agra, he conquered large territories and established the Mughal empire.

Babur's grandson, Akbar (1556–1605), one of the greatest Mughal rulers, spent the 40 years of his reign establishing an empire that encompassed the greater part of northern India. He held court in Delhi, Agra and Lahore, and built the lovely fortified royal palace at Fatehpur Sikri, near Agra. The workshops at Akbar's court attracted artists from all over the empire, and great painters and craftsmen from Persia and other neighbouring countries came to seek their fortune.

Akbar's son, Jahangir, inherited the empire, which he ruled with moderate success. But it was Jahangir's son and heir, Shah Jahan, who had many credits to his name, not least the construction of the Taj Mahal. Inheriting a vast empire, Shah Jahan succeeded in maintaining and adding to it. He also spent time redeveloping his capitals at Lahore and Agra, and in 1638 began the construction of a new capital city in Delhi.

EUROPEAN SETTLEMENTS

By the mid-17th century the East India companies of England, France, Denmark and the Netherlands began obtaining trading rights in India. The home countries amassed great wealth from the sale of cheaply available silk, cotton, indigo, spices and timber for shipbuilding from the Indian subcontinent. In exchange, the traders brought curios from the west and paid in gold and silver for their commercial transactions. The rivalry between these countries soon became quite intense, each seeking to dominate the European market through successful plunder of the east.

By 1640, the British East India Company, involved in trade with India and the Far East, established their fort in Chennai in southern India. They had gained trading rights from the local rulers who also benefited to some extent from the vast amount of money that was being made on the export of goods to Europe. The forts in Chennai and in Surat in the west, and the creation of the town of Kolkota in eastern India in 1690 saw the entrenchment of British interests.

By the beginning of the 18th century, the Mughal empire had begun to disintegrate. With the resulting power struggles in the north and unrest among the kingdoms further south, India's political climate became increasingly unsettled.

The British and the French found themselves obliged to protect their own trading interests. They built up their companies, raised their own armies and developed administrative systems. Gradually the British grew in power, and the French became isolated in the Pondicherry region in the south. At this time, the Dutch East India Company had moved from India to Indonesia.

The British played politics with local rulers and in Bengal gained control of revenue collection. This new development was replicated in all other areas under British influence in the Indian subcontinent, to their advantage. Revenue collection meant that the East India Company could pay for commodities in India without bringing gold out from England. Soon, British interests were being paid for by the colony, to the benefit of the company as well as private investors and traders.

Towards the end of the 18th century the East India Company set in motion plans for deeper penetration and control of the subcontinent. Roads and bridges were built and investments in improving the distribution and collection networks organized. Ship-building yards were set up, railways established in 1853, and telegraph and postal systems planned. Some social reforms and an English form of education were also introduced.

However, the Indian economy suffered considerably, with the extortion of heavy taxes, adverse terms of trade, and limited interest in improving agricultural practices and welfare measures. The import of cheap post-industrial revolution goods from England crippled Indian industry.

The safety valve blew in 1857, and for a year and a half Indian soldiers of the British army mutinied against their white rulers. City after city in north India witnessed spontaneous uprisings, both sides massacring men, women and children. The British army managed to quell the mutiny and crush the uprising, but in so doing opened a new chapter in the history of British India.

THE BRITISH EMPIRE

In 1858, Indian territory was transferred from the hands of the East India Company to the British Crown by an Act of Parliament. The threat of a recurrence of violence and the disruption of trade and revenue collection greatly alarmed the British, and new laws were enforced. As a result, Indians were allowed to occupy only subordinate ranks in the army and civil services. Measures were also initiated to eliminate or subordinate local rulers, giving the British unchallenged control of the subcontinent.

The empire builders began work in setting their colony in order. Roads were built, bridges constructed. The universities of Mumbai, Chennai and Kolkota were founded in 1857. British law, administrative and judicial systems were introduced throughout the colony. Industry, trading houses and banks were established and large tracts of virgin land

The British East India Company commissioned numerous 'Company' artists to record daily life in India. This painting depicts the swarree *or royal procession of one of the last Mughal emperors, Akbar the Second, who reigned from 1806 to 1837.*

Between 1858 and Independence, India was 'the jewel in the crown' of Britain's empire. Numerous alliances were made with local rulers, and royal visits to the country were accompanied by much pomp and splendour. In 1876 the then Prince of Wales visited Rajasthan. Here, in this huge painting (4.9 x 6.7 metres/ 16 x 22 feet), by Vassily Verestchagin, the Prince and Ram Singh, the Maharaja of Jaipur, are shown in procession on elephant back through the streets of Jaipur.

were converted into British-owned plantations to grow tea and coffee for export.

The tightening control over the British Empire in India saw the beginnings of a new movement towards independence. In 1885 an organization of British-educated intellectuals and members of the elite formed the Indian National Congress, to participate in their country's destiny. Although united in their goal, these reformers were, in fact, a disparate group of 'moderates', 'extremists' and 'reformists' seeking divergent solutions to India's problems.

In 1905 the British planned the division of Bengal for purposes of administration. The division unfortunately fell into a pattern that divided east Bengal, with a Muslim majority, from west Bengal, with a Hindu majority. This hidden agenda was quickly seized upon by the people of Bengal who launched a major resistance movement to British rule. There were strikes and demonstrations and the call went out to boycott British goods. Great bonfires were lit, burning the British imported goods that had so severely crippled the Indian economy, an action of resistance that hit at the very heart of British rule in India. With the use of police and military force the movement was quelled but it laid the foundation of the National movement that eventually liberated India.

In 1911, the British chose Delhi rather than Kolkota, Mumbai or Chennai as the capital of the British Empire in India. The foundation stone was laid in a ceremony full of pomp and splendour by King George V and Queen Mary. Work started on the building of a new capital city, New Delhi, beside the seven other known historic cities and forts.

STRUGGLE FOR FREEDOM

In 1915 Mohandas Karmachand Gandhi, affectionately called Gandhiji or Mahatma, 'the great soul', returned to India from South Africa where he had organized the Indian and Black population to fight the repressive and inhuman policy of apartheid enforced by the state. Gandhi was soon involved in the freedom struggle. He understood that India was largely an agricultural nation, that the village was the basic economic and social unit, and strove to build a self-sufficient economy that would restore the unity and balance shattered by colonial economy. It was his ardent desire and, indeed, profound belief that freedom should and could be won only by peaceful resistance, using the powerful weapon of non-cooperation, and, above all else, avoiding any form of violence.

Unfortunately, events belied his dream. There were militant Indians determined to seize power through force, believing it to be the only effective way. There were innumerable occasions when peaceful demon-

strations ended with thousands of casualties and deaths. Gandhi fasted, protested, parleyed with British officials but never wavered in his resolve to conduct a non-violent struggle against colonial rule, often calling off movements that threatened to become violent. His non-cooperation movement gathered tremendous support from the people, who followed him devoutly, giving mass support to every call to challenge British authority. Civil disobedience, or non-compliance with unjust laws, was one of the key forms of resistance.

When the Second World War broke out India fought beside the British to bring an end to Fascism in Germany, Italy and Japan. This common enemy brought ruler and the ruled into temporary partnership. With the end of the war, however, the Indian freedom movement intensified and reached its final stage. The British parliament was obliged to concede transfer of power to India. Increasing unrest was exacerbated by intercommunal violence as the Muslim League, headed by Muhammad Ali Jinnah, pressed for a separate Muslim state. In a last and very painful gamble to retain control the British exploited these internal factional rivalries, dividing Hindus from Muslims, and leaders from their supporters.

Much to the anguish of Gandhi and his followers, it was decided that India would be partitioned into two countries, India and Pakistan, on the basis of religious majority. One portion

Modern India's two great early leaders: Mahatma Gandhi (left), *the advocate of non-violent resistance, united his people against colonial rule; Jawaharlal Nehru* (right), *Gandhi's choice as India's first Prime Minister, founded the Nehru-Gandhi political dynasty.*

of Pakistan lay to the west, separated by the Indian Gangetic plains from East Pakistan, where a sizeable Muslim community lived. News of this partition on the basis of religion caused waves of fear, millions of Muslims sought asylum in Pakistan territory and Hindus fled to India in search of refuge. The consequences were catastrophic — enormous bloodshed, with millions of families on either side of the border uprooted, the victims of murder, violence and looting, as they sought to find new homes and new lives in alien surroundings.

On 15 August 1947, the last Viceroy, Lord Mountbatten, handed over the reins of government and India became independent. Gandhi, to the last working for a return to peace, was assassinated by a Hindu extremist early the following year.

GOVERNMENT

The Indian Constitution, drawn up after Independence, came into force on 26 January 1950. The Constitution describes India as a union of states, a Sovereign Socialist Secular Democratic Republic, with a parliamentary form of government. The formal head of the union and supreme commander of its armed forces is the President of India. He resides in Rashtrapati Bhavan, the grand mansion designed for the British Viceroy. Real executive power lies with an elected council of ministers, headed by the

Prime Minister. The council of ministers is answerable to the House of the People, the Lok Sabha, members of parliament elected on the basis of universal franchise. The upper house of parliament, called the Rajya Sabha, the Council of States, consists of members indirectly elected by members of state assemblies and members of parliament.

Each state within the union is headed by a governor appointed by the Central Government and the executive council of ministers, with a chief minister nominated by the majority party, responsible to the legislative assembly of members.

India has 28 states and seven union territories, each with their own legislative assembly, represented in the Lok Sabha by elected members. The Lok Sabha has a maximum of 550 members, the Rajya Sabha a maximum of 250. The term of office of both Lok Sabha and Council of Ministers is five years unless it is dissolved.

GOVERNMENT SINCE INDEPENDENCE
The party that has dominated the Indian electoral scene has been the Indian National Congress Party, founded in 1885, which spearheaded the Indian freedom struggle. Jawaharlal Nehru was elected to serve as India's first Prime Minister. He was Gandhi's choice and the combination of an English education and a passionate knowledge of, and belief in, India's intellectual and cultural heritage provided a sound basis for the role. Influenced by socialist principles, Nehru's policy of building up the industrial infrastructure through enormous direct government investment has been criticized for giving insufficient attention to rural development.

Nehru died in 1964 and was succeeded for a brief spell by Lal Bahadur Shastri. In 1966, Indira Gandhi, the only child and daughter of Nehru, became Prime Minister, winning resounding victories in the first few elections. In 1971, East Pakistan rebelled against Pakistan and, in the struggle to

establish its sovereignty as Bangladesh, was supported by Mrs Gandhi directing the Indian army, which played a prominent role in the creation of this independent country.

In 1975, Mrs Gandhi was found guilty of electoral corruption. For two years she clung to power by imposing restrictions on the press and declaring a state of internal emergency. In 1977, when she stood for re-election, she was resoundingly defeated. The Janata Party came to power with Moraji Desai as Prime Minister, and with Congress as the majority opposition party. In the 1980 elections Mrs Gandhi returned to power and remained Prime Minister until her assassination in 1984.

The Congress Party, in a crisis of leadership chose Indira Gandhi's son, Rajiv, as the next Prime Minister. This 40-year-old grandson of Jawaharlal Nehru had trained as an airline pilot and until his mother's death had shown little interest in politics.

In 1989, heading a government wrecked by bribery scandal, Rajiv Gandhi lost the elections. For another short spell the opposition leader V.P. Singh was elected Prime Minister. In the late 1980s, Sri Lankan separatists were conducting a militant campaign to establish an independent country, and many refugees sought asylum in India. Rajiv Gandhi sent a peace-keeping force to Sri Lanka, a move which possibly sealed his fate. In May 1991, while campaigning in Tamil Nadu for the General Election, he was assassinated, it is believed, at the hands of extremist Sri Lankan

Tamil separatists.

Narasimha Rao, a senior member of the Congress Party who had served as a cabinet minister for a number of years, was then elected Prime Minister. For the first time since Independence, the Congress Party no longer had a member of the Nehru-Gandhi family at the helm. Mr Rao successfully completed his five-year term, with the Congress holding a majority of seats in parliament. The largest opposition group was the Bharatiya Janata Party (BJP), which has been criticized for its right-wing Hindu fundamentalist politics. In the May 1996 general elections both Congress and the BJP suffered a setback. The Indian electorate gave none of the major contenders a clear mandate, and voted out of power those leaders who had been accused of misconduct and misuse of power. While the BJP had the largest and the Congress the next largest number of seats in parliament, neither had a clear-cut majority. After the 1999 elections India's central government was led by the BJP, with support from an amalgam of smaller parties. Rajiv Gandhi's Italian-born wife, Sonia, took his place as the head of the Congress Party and became leader of the Opposition in parliament. In the May 2004 general elections, Sonia Gandhi led the Congress Party to a surprise election win. However, she turned down the position of Prime Minister, allowing Manmohan Singh, Finance Minister in Mr Rao's government, to take over the reins. At the time of writing, Congress had the support of some 320 MPs in the 543-member house.

ECONOMY

Building up the economy of a large nation such as India has presented the government with a challenging task. Roads and transport networks of various kinds had to be established throughout the country. The Indian Railways are the principal (and often the cheapest) mode of transporting freight and people. Since the first steam engine was flagged off in Mumbai in 1853,

the country has established a network of over 7,000 railway stations and tracks that extend over a distance of 62,000 kilometres (39,000 miles) today. Post and telecommunication systems were set up throughout the country and now India's own satellites have changed the face of its communication networks.

AGRICULTURE

The agricultural sector provides livelihood to 70 per cent of the Indian labour force. This includes the small-scale farmer, hired labour and owners of large plantations. Agriculture also provides up to 32 per cent of the Net National Product and accounts for a large share of the country's exports in the form of tea and coffee. Since Independence the

Originally designed for the Viceroy in the days of British imperial rule, Rashtrapati Bhavan in New Delhi is now the President of India's official residence.

government has made efforts to release the poor farmer from debts and age-old feudal practices. A series of land and tenancy reforms, loans and financial aid to farmers has made some difference to their life of hardship, while they toil to feed the nation.

Much of the land under agriculture is fed by the monsoon rains, the vagaries of which cause havoc when flooding or drought occur. Large irrigation programmes and the channelling of rivers to feed the land have not proved as successful as traditional land-use practices. The development of high-yielding varieties of seeds in the 1970s had a dramatic effect on wheat production in India, turning the country from a net importer of food grain to self-sufficiency. This so-called 'green revolution' did not equally affect the cultivation of rice, which continues to be the most intensively grown crop in India and forms the staple diet of most of the people. Wheat is grown mainly in north India, along with other cereals. For a largely poor population, pulses are a key part of the diet. After Brazil and China, India is the world's largest vegetable and fruit producer.

The protein intake of the poor is still largely derived from milk-based products such as curds. A number of farmers also rear small herds of goats and cattle which provide the bare necessities. In coastal and riverine areas such as Goa, Kerala and Orissa, fishing and fish products form an important part of the economy.

ENERGY

Large-scale electrification programmes to provide every Indian village with electric lighting have been a major government concern. Enormous power plants have been built and hydroelectric projects developed throughout the country.

In both rural and urban societies, fuel requirements are still met by firewood and cow dung. The depletion of wood and forests has caused severe environmental problems, but without an alternative source of fuel, villagers have to suffer great hardship. In some areas, women have to walk for three or four hours to gather enough firewood to cook the day's meal. The damage to the environment and the increasing demand for sources of energy such as coal, gas and wood has led many non-government organizations to work towards finding sustainable alternatives.

TEXTILES

The textile industry is the single largest organized sector in India and employs over 11,000,000 workers. India has, over the centuries, produced very fine cotton fabrics, although this industry suffered a severe set-back during the British period. The recovery during the last couple of decades has been remarkable, and Indian textiles form a major component of its export business. Besides cotton, jute and silk are major cottage industries.

INDUSTRY

Nehru's economic policy, which steered a line between capitalism and socialism, was euphemistically termed 'democratic socialism'. It resulted in heavy investments in public sector undertakings, to keep under state control what were termed the 'commanding heights' of the economy. Transport, railway and airline systems, large-scale industries, electricity, gas, postal and telegraph systems

and a host of others, were government-run. To these were added a number of unrelated consumer industries. Special laws protected these public-sector undertakings and the result was the growth of a crippling bureaucratic system, with its repercussions—bribery, corruption and inefficiency.

The restricted import policy of the last 45 years has seen the growth of a healthy, competitive middle class, an industrial ethos and small-scale industries that today produce a mass of consumer items within India. The restrictions on imports and the policy of self-reliance kept India out of the foreign debt that has ruined many a developing country.

In 1993, under Narasimha Rao's and subsequent governments, relaxation of import policies and foreign investments in India has opened the doors to multinational corporations. The question now being debated is whether these multinationals will, as they have done in other third-world countries, lead to the ruin of the environment and corrode the cultural heritage of this ancient country.

ARTS AND CRAFTS

Among the most remarkable features of Indian culture, and the arts in particular, are its antiquity and continuity. Most cultures of the world have lost the continuity of their

artistic tradition. In India, the performing and visual arts are based on an in-built system of creativity and innovation, and for this reason have endured for centuries, remaining authentic and never monotonous. Whether a housewife is painting symbolic motifs on the walls of her mud home, or a musician is singing in the classical Carnatic music tradition, improvisation and creativity are fundamental to their art. No two renderings of music or dance performances are ever the same; no wall painting or embroidery is ever repeated; no two temples are identical. This continuity has been facilitated by the family, the caste system and the characteristic qualities of Indian aesthetics.

Another unique feature is the integration within the arts in India. The same mythological story is rendered in music, dance, painting, a temple festival and embroidery. The code or symbolic representations that appear on a Buddhist *thanka* or hand-painted scroll also appear on wall paintings and sculptures and on masks used for ritual dances. Unlike the European tradition, the arts of India, both performing and visual, literary and religious, are integrated to a great extent. Along with this is the extraordinary wealth and diversity of styles that exist in all forms of artistic expression.

MUSIC

Every state in India has a different language and a different style of music. In every Indian language, there is devotional and ritual music, as well as seasonal songs and dance to accompany harvest or sowing of the new crop. There are work songs, to be sung while pounding rice, and social songs related to the life-cycle of a human being, for example to celebrate birth or marriage.

This ancient tradition of singing still continues in the rural areas, to the accompaniment of an assortment of musical instruments. India has a wide variety of drums: vertical (*tabla*), horizontal, one-sided, two-sided, those that are slung on the neck and played, those that are too heavy to lift up and carry. There are several types of stringed instruments, from the single-wired *ektara* to the complex *sitar*, a many-stringed fretted instrument. Wind instruments are as varied, with flutes, double pipes, metal horns, bamboo flutes, reed instruments and a host of others. There are bells, cymbals, gongs and

The agricultural sector is India's largest employer. Over 75 million tonnes of rice are cultivated each year, mostly for home consumption. The paddy fields shown here are in Andhra Pradesh.

clappers. Some forms of regional music are played only on certain instruments and distinct instruments are associated with special festivals or rituals, such as the conch for Hindu temple worship, and the long horns or *nagaswarams* for processions and marriages.

Singing and playing at social and religious occasions, festivals and marriages, at work and at play are a form of bonding for the family and the community. The music is not written down but is spontaneous and vibrant, changing as new members join the group, each contributing his or her talents to ensure that family traditions are passed on.

Another tradition to be found in all parts of India is the singing of ballads by the village storyteller, or professional storytellers, to narrate myths about gods and goddesses, and to describe the lives of local, historical heroes. Often the storyteller makes use of a scroll painting to illustrate the main events of the ballad, and these may vary from the beautiful hand-painted scrolls of Rajasthan, called *Bhapuji ka phad*, to the comic-book-like scroll of the *Patta Chitra* of eastern India.

The notes of the sitar *and the improvisations of the* raga *may sum up the sound of India to Western ears, but the country has innumerable musical styles, such as the regional music played in Rajasthan.*

Apart from rural and regional forms, there are two broad systems of classical music, Hindustani of northern India and Carnatic, which is popular in the states of Karnataka, Tamil Nadu, Andhra Pradesh and Kerala. Both traditions have roots in rural and tribal music and appear to have evolved from ancient religious music and chanting.

The basis of the Indian classical music tradition is the *raga*, a system of scales set to different time-cycles called *talas*. The melodic pattern of the *raga* is governed by a strict code of elaboration, allowing for improvisation and creativity every time it is sung. There are no score sheets, or written *ragas*, but great masters of improvisation are renowned for their compositions.

DANCE AND DRAMA

Dance in India is just as much a part of life as music. Every state and every community within a state has its own tradition of dances for festivals, religious rituals or social events like marriages. India has a population of twenty million tribals and each community has its own unique contribution to make.

The huge repertoire of regional and tribal dances would be almost impossible to quantify, but in Indian classical dance, six forms are recognized. *Bharatnatyam* is popular throughout India, especially in Tamil Nadu, in the south, where it originated. It is a solo dance item, now performed mainly by women. The style is loved for the purity of its angular, energetic lines. *Odissi* was once performed in the temples of Orissa, in eastern India. The dance places emphasis on lyrical movements and curves of the body, with flowing lines of semicircles and circles in both movements and compositions. *Kuchipudi* originated in a small village of the same name in the state of Andhra Pradesh. It is essentially a dance-drama with many characters who portray Hindu myths and legends. The *Kathak* dance of northern India was said to have evolved from an ancient storytelling tradition. The performer narrates myths and religious poetry using subtle hand gestures and facial expressions. In the medieval period, the dance evolved further as a court dance with fast footwork and pirouettes. There are two styles of dressing, the long, gathered skirt, blouse and head cover, or Muslim-type dress with tight pyjamas. The dancer wears many ankle bells, for much emphasis falls on the footwork of *Kathak*.

Manipuri is the classical dance form from the easternmost state of Manipur, close to the Myanmar (Burma) border. The many items in the repertoire include martial dance with swords and shields and performers dancing and drumming at the same time. The most beautiful item is *Ras*, with female dancers dressed in stiff, long skirts studded with sequins and embroidery. The head is covered with a delicate, transparent veil. Famed for its grace, gentle, tiny foot movements and flowing lines created by rotating wrists and arms, this dance has a distinctive east Asian flavour and charm.

The *Kathakali* style originated from ancient Sanskrit dance-dramas and depicts the epic poems of the *Ramayana* and *Mahabharata* in all their splendour. In *Kathakali*, make-up is an art in itself, with vegetable and natural colours carefully prepared and applied to the face, each colour having its own coded message — green for good, red and black for evil. The dancer-actors perform through the night for several nights. The stage has no props, a mere hand-held curtain signifies a change of scene. The entire performance is carried out by the light of oil lamps and to live music, with a singer, drummer and percussionists.

Classical dancers require years of training and a deep knowledge of music and literature before they can perform. It is rare for a dancer to be proficient in more than one style. These classical dance forms have a strict grammar, a codified body language of elaborate hand gestures and intricate foot movements, and distinctive choreography, costume and style. Yet they all comprise two essential integrated parts, the *nritya* or pure dance and *abhinaya,* drama or mime. In a dance-drama, the performer will punctuate the recital with pure dance items to exhibit intricacies of the style, using body and foot movements in particular.

In Kerala, the only Sanskrit drama style still preserved is *Kudiyattam,* but there are other ritual performances such as *Theyyam,* where the participants wear huge symbolic masks and headgear and serve in the role of the deity to bless and consecrate the ritual. Among other important dance-drama forms are *Yakshagana* from Karnataka and *Chauu* of eastern India in which the players use elaborate make-up or masks, wear exaggerated costumes and tell mythological stories. Further rural and regional forms include *Ram Lila* of northern India, which tells the story of the *Ramayana.* It is a complete theatre form with audience participation and movement to different locations. It is performed over many nights leading to the end of a festival.

A substantial amount of work is being done to document these amazing dance, drama and ritual forms. What role they will play in contemporary society outside their rural, economic and religious contex, is still a major question. Yet many contemporary theatre groups are using these roots for inspiration, as traditional music, dance and drama have much to offer modern audiences.

LITERATURE
Each region in India has evolved its own dialect, script and literature. There is a great oral tradition through which poetry and other literary forms were passed from one generation to the next. In ancient India, Sanskrit was the language of the elite, used for religious texts, court literature and poetry. One of old India's most famous poet-dramatists, Kalidasa, is still held in high regard. His works

In the classical Odissi *dance of Orissa, the performers make lyrical movements that have their origins in temple dances. The richly decorated costumes are made of the woven* ikat *cloth so popular in eastern India.*

include the lyrical love-story of Shakuntula and Kumarsambhava. Tamil literature of the Sangam period is equally famous. Epic poems such as the *Ramayana* and the *Mahabharata* were composed over a period of time, and there are several other language versions in present-day India.

During the medieval period, many Indian languages developed a storehouse of their own literature. Around AD 1000, Persian and Arabic influenced trends in Indian literature. Great Sufi poets and scholars created religious and secular texts. Urdu, a synthesis of Hindustani and Persian, became the language of the poets in the mid-15th century. *Bhakti* poetry, like the Sufi tradition, sang of the love of the human soul for the divine. Poems of Kabir, a Muslim, and the female poetess

Mirabhai are popular, even today.

During the colonial period, English writing informed the world about India and its classical literary and religious works through translations and studies. Inspired by the freedom movement, Indian writers began to compose literary works in both their own mother tongue and in English. The poems of Rabindranath Tagore, India's only poet laureate, are representative of this effervescence of Indian writing. Since Independence many Indian novelists and poets write in English, like R.K. Narayan, Ved Metha, Anita Desai and Vikram Seth, who have made a distinct contribution to world literature.

ARCHITECTURE
Famous buildings in India tend to be historical religious structures, forts and palaces. This is because large-scale monumental construction projects required heavy finances and royal patronage. This is not to suggest that there is no worthwhile domestic secular architectural tradition in India. Some village homes are valuable architectural designs. Built to suit climatic conditions, they are both environmentally sound and aesthetically and emotionally pleasing.

A major event in Indian architectural terms came with the birth of Buddhism. Sanchi, not far from Bhopal in Madhya Pradesh, has some of the earliest Buddhist monuments or *stupas,* the most important of which is said to contain the remains of the Buddha in the centre of its solid mound. The semicircular form of this shrine represents the *anda,* the egg from which new spiritual life will grow. The *stupa* is surrounded by a stone railing with four gateways or *toran* facing the cardinal directions (each gate is 8.5 metres/28 feet high). It is on the *toran* that some of the finest early Buddhist sculpture is to be found, depicting Buddhist symbols and scenes from the *Jatakas,* tales of the life of the Buddha. Amaravati and Nagarjunakonda in Andhra Pradesh are also well-known early Buddhist pilgrimage centres.

Ajanta, in Maharashtra, is an extraordinary site, located on a horseshoe-shaped hillside on the bend of a river. Cutting into the cliff face, Buddhist monks and artisans excavated huge prayer halls and dormitories for their religious order. The entire wall surfaces of these rooms in the hill were embellished with sculptural decorations, then painted.

The most important religious structure for the Hindus is the temple. The temple complex grew from modest beginnings, probably in wood and bamboo, to huge structures carved out of the living rock, such as those found in Mahabalipuram in Tamil Nadu, Badami and Aihole in Karnataka, and Ellora in Maharashtra. Between the 7th and the 13th centuries every region of India had its own style of temple building, though all were united by form and religious content. Some of the splendid examples of Bhubaneshwar and Puri, in Orissa, are still used for worship, while the amazing temple at Konarak,

designed to resemble the chariot of the sun god, stands deserted. In northern India, the finest surviving temples of the 10th century are those found at Khajuraho in Madhya Pradesh, famous for their monumental architecture and fine statues and equally infamous for the erotic sculptures on the walls.

With the introduction of Islam into India, a new set of architectural requirements had to be met by the local artisan. What evolved was a spectacular synthesized style termed Indo-Islamic architecture. The most important buildings during this period were mosques for prayer, larger mosques (called Jama or Juma Masjids) for congregational Friday prayers, tombs to bury the dead and fortified palaces for the rulers.

Though there are many examples of how the style evolved in different regions of India, maturity of form and function and great

beauty were attained in the Mughal period. One of the most notable Mughal rulers, Shah Jahan, built the Taj Mahal at Agra as a tomb for his favourite wife. This amazing building is set in a garden, representing the garden of paradise. The tomb is completely faced with white marble and decorated with sculptured panels and inlay work. In Delhi, Shah Jahan built the Red Fort, a 17th-century fortified palace with elaborately decorated rooms and ornamental gardens. He also built the classic Friday mosque, the Jama Masjid in Delhi.

While the Mughals dominated a large portion of India, other rulers continued their artistic traditions in different parts of the country. In Rajasthan, mighty forts and ornate palaces were built by famous rulers. Some of these have now been converted into hotels such as the Lake Palace in Udaipur, set on an island in the lake.

Religious patronage has been responsible for much of India's architectural heritage. The same holds true today. The fine Buddhist stupa *at Sanchi* (above) *was originally built in the 3rd century* BC. *Two millennia later, New Delhi's spectacular Lotus Temple* (above right) *was built in the early 1980s by the Baha'i faithful.*

Royal patronage was responsible for India's great secular buildings, today a role taken on by big business. In Rajasthan, fabulous palaces and hilltop forts with lavish interiors, such as those in Jodhpur's Meherangarh Fort (right), *were built by the Maharajas. Jai Singh of Jaipur went further: he also planned his pink city and, in 1728, constructed the extraordinary Jantar Mantar astronomical observatory* (far right).

During the early colonial period several British forts were built at important trading centres such as Fort St George in Chennai, and Fort William in Kolkota. Impressive railway stations, administrative buildings and colonial houses were built around the country. When Delhi was chosen to be the capital of the British Empire in India, a huge project was initiated. The chief architects were Sir Edwin Lutyens and Sir Herbert Baker and the city was conceived in a composite style, with features from Imperial Greece and Rome, European and Indian architecture.

Efforts are being made to preserve India's rich architectural heritage, but it is an ongoing race against development and insensitive planning. The Archaeological Survey of India is in charge of the preservation of over 5,000 buildings in the country while state governments look after a few thousand more. Yet the number of protected monuments needs to be enlarged to encompass more regional styles and some ancient cityscapes and historical towns. Today, the question of pollution, vibration of air traffic and other environmental issues are threatening the conservation of important historical sites, including the Taj Mahal. The monuments of India need to be preserved, for they are a part of the world's cultural heritage.

PAINTING

The earliest examples of Indian art are the work of Stone Age cave-dwellers whose paintings, the oldest dating back to over 5,000 years BC, still survive on the rock walls of their primitive homes. Crude but lively, they were executed in a wide range of natural pigments, depicting hunting scenes with large wild animals like the bull and stick figures engaged in ritual activities.

No other evidence now remains of the development of Indian painting in the last few centuries BC, but by the 5th century AD cave murals had reached a very different level of sophistication. In the great Buddhist cave-temple systems at Ajanta, in Maharashtra, the world's finest examples of religious wall-paintings cover the surfaces of chamber after chamber with astonishingly well-crafted scenes from Buddhist lore, the soft mineral colours retaining their richness down the ages. In the Deccan, fragments of 6th-century Hindu, Buddhist and Jain cave-temple murals show the influence of south Indian painting, using few, but strong colours.

On a smaller scale, the palm-leaf miniatures of the medieval east Indian Pala dynasty echo something of the style of Ajanta. These paintings illuminated Buddhist texts, written on palm leaves sewn between wooden covers, and exhibited exquisite nuances of colour and line. In contrast, the palm-leaf paintings of the Jains in western India were more angular and stylized, the colours bold and simple.

The supreme flowering of Indian painting came with the rise to power of the Mughal dynasty in the 16th century. These great patrons of the arts brought Persian artists to their courts. Under their guidance, a school of painting was created that produced India's most glorious pictorial records of history, mythology, court life, landscapes and natural history. Representing the epitome of Mughal art are the miniature illustrations decorating books and albums from the reigns of Akbar and his son, Jahangir. New pigments, a refined understanding of colour and perspective, superb brushwork and stunning achievements of realism resulted in a contribution to art that has scarcely been rivalled since.

Other important schools of Indian miniature painting were those of the states of Rajasthan, Punjab and the Himalayan foothills. Although these were, at least in their later periods, influenced by the Mughal style, they were more illusive and symbolic, representing ideals and illustrating episodes from the lives of the gods as allegories of the human soul's passage to wisdom.

With the predominance of European interests in the subcontinent, the excellence of

The exquisite miniature paintings produced by artists under the patronage of the Mughal rulers depicted everything from daily life in the imperial court to flora and fauna. Influenced by Mughal techniques, but concentrating on symbolic themes, a separate school of fine miniature painting evolved in Rajasthan (above). Today, modern miniatures are still painted in traditional styles (left).

miniature painting began to decline. Although officials of the British East India Company commissioned local artists to produce paintings and drawings as a record of what they considered to be the essential India (costumes, festivals, plants and animals), these lacked the purity and vibrancy of the past. But some of the so-called Company Paintings are interesting for their mixture of styles, and have their own merits.

Today, India has a thriving contemporary art scene. Painters such as M.F. Hussain, Bendre, Bhupen Khakar and Ghulam Sheik, with their own media and styles, are firmly established in the international art world.

HANDICRAFTS

Each area or region in India has specialized crafts depending on the availability of natural material: clay, precious and semi-precious stones, metal and wood. Such crafts have a long history because of their inherent value, the perfection of the design and its function.

Clay objects and toys found at archaeological sites suggest that the art of pottery in India is more than 5,000 years old. Today, red, black and grey pottery similar to these ancient artefacts is still being produced for water storage vessels, cooking utensils and toys. Stonework is equally famous and as ancient a craft. Different types of stone found in particular regions were used to construct religious buildings for Buddhists, Hindus, Jains, Muslims and Christians. Sandstone Buddhist monuments of the 2nd century BC in central India had finely detailed sculptured reliefs, and the granite Hindu shrines of Tamil Nadu of the 6th century AD had enormous stone sculptural decorations. The soft soapstone of Orissa and the hard grey granite of Tamil Nadu are still used in the 21st century to make sculptural items.

In Agra, in northern India, there are craftsmen still proficient in preparing stone inlay work with designs very like those used on the Taj Mahal. Inlay work is usually set into white marble, the design being cut into the surface of the stone and filled in with semi-precious gems. The value of the inlay increases in direct proportion to the number of inlaid stones. On the royal tombs of the Taj Mahal over 50 different gems were used to create a single flower.

Jewellery and gem-cutting work is also one of the prides of Indian craft. Jaipur, in

Handicrafts flourish in every corner of India. For the acquisitive visitor, the choice can be overwhelming: silver and gold jewellery, gemstones, inlaid marble work, brass and copper ware, silk carpets and wool rugs, painted papier mâché, toys and puppets, wood and stone carving, furniture, pottery and ceramic ware, fans, marquetry and lacquer, paintings, miniatures and wall hangings, leatherware, flutes and other musical instruments, fabrics, textiles and clothing of all kinds – the list is endless.

Rajasthan, Surat in Gujarat, and south India are famous gem centres. A wide variety of gemstones – agate, garnet, quartz and topaz – are cut and set in traditional craft shops. The silver jewellery of Rajasthan is very popular today, while the gold jewellery of southern India has a unique style and elegance. Every region has its own speciality which the connoisseur can identify.

Metal and alloys such as bronze, brass and bell metal were also used in ancient societies to make vessels for storage or decorative ware. Images in bronze date back to the Harappan period – the famous 'Dancing Girl' in Delhi's National Museum is evidence of this sophisticated art form. Buddhist and Hindu images of deities were made by the *cire perdue* or 'lost wax' technique. In this process, wax models were prepared and then set into

a mud mould, the wax was melted and removed and molten metal was poured into the mould. When cooled, the metal took the form of the wax model, retaining its fluid lines. Tribal metalware from Dogra utilizes a similar technique but here the wax is rolled into thin threads and wound round to make objects. The rope-like texture is retained in the finished metal product, giving it its identifiable form. One can buy brass figurines, water jars and other metal objects of every kind almost anywhere in India.

Wood is also used to make many household items and furniture. In south India, where lovely rosewood, teak and other fine woods are available, tables and decorative boxes, intricately carved and inlaid, are made with a high degree of skill. It is wise for tourists to enquire about the origins of such articles as some tree species, especially sandalwood, are endangered and now protected by law.

DRESS AND FABRICS

Every region, community, caste and religion has its own preferred textile and style of dressing. Until quite recently, one could tell by the clothes they wore where people came from and to which community they belonged. Cotton shawls with distinct geometric designs for each tribe are made in the states of Nagaland, Meghalaya and Tripura. In Rajasthan, Gujarat and tribal communities of Andhra Pradesh, women wear ankle-length billowing skirts decorated with embroidery and tiny mirrors. In northern India, after the influence of Islamic culture, stitched pyjamas and *kurta,* or knee-length shirts, are worn by men and women. In eastern and southern India, where the climate determines light clothing, women wear sarong-like cloths wrapped around the lower body. *Saris* are single length fabrics of 5.5 metres (16½ feet) long worn by women, each region having its distinct styles and texture. Men wear *dhotis* or single-piece cloths wound around the lower torso in a variety of styles. A favourite tourist purchase is the *bandhgala,* literally a coat 'closed at the throat', also known as a 'Nehru' jacket.

Very fine cotton is grown in Gujarat and peninsular India. Camel-hair wool is used in Rajasthan and Gujarat to make colourful shawls and household items. The finest woollen shawls come from Kashmir and Himachal Pradesh; the priceless *Shahtush* shawls are now prohibited by law as a means to protect this rare species.

Silk is a relatively new material in India. Some tribal communities in Assam, Orissa and Madhya Pradesh use raw silk to make shawls and other clothes. Rough and unevenly spun by hand, it has a characteristic textured look. There is a legend that silk was originally smuggled into India from China, but it was introduced on a large scale by the French in Karnataka between the 17th and 18th centuries. The silk weavers in Karnataka and Tamil Nadu favour bright colours, with contrasting borders and woven motifs. Silk brocade is produced in the area of Varanasi in

Marriage ceremonies in India are the occasion for finery. In this procession in Jaipur, the young bridegroom sits astride a horse, itself elaborately decorated.

Uttar Pradesh. During the weaving process, tiny shuttles introduce gold and silver motifs into the fabric.

Once a fabric is woven, there are various techniques to further embellish and decorate the material. Wood-block hand-printed fabrics are famous in Rajasthan and Gujarat. A wooden block crafted with part of the design is used for one colour printing, then subsequent blocks, with separate colours, are stamped on to the cloth until the motif is complete. Textiles printed with many colours and tiny motifs are examples of the skill of the artists.

Bhandani, or tie and dye, is another craft of Rajasthan and Gujarat. Here, sections of white fabric are tied with thread to create a design and the cloth is dyed, the knotted areas resisting the dye. Further sections are then tied for subsequent dyeing. At the end of the process, the knots are opened to reveal a cloth of multi-coloured patterns. Such designs are used to decorate the long bright cloths that make turbans for men and veils for women.

Popular in eastern India, Andhra Pradesh and Gujarat are *ikat* fabrics, produced by a

complex weaving and dyeing technique that is also found in other Asian countries. At their best, such textiles may take years to complete, as they involve an intricate and highly skilled process in which the threads are tie-dyed in sections before being woven.

Textiles can also be embellished with embroidery and appliqué work. The cloth appliqué or patchwork of Rajasthan, Gujarat and Orissa is the most beautiful, with colourful motifs of scenes from everyday life added to quilts and clothes. Embroidery can range from the very sophisticated and expensive to amusing novelties. There is a tradition of gold-thread embroidery or *zari* work which is applied to silk, cotton and woollen shawls, shirts and fabrics. The embroiderers of Agra and Lucknow in Uttar Pradesh, Hyderabad in Andhra Pradesh and Delhi produce incredible wedding outfits covered with silver or gold threadwork and coloured sequins.

Valiant efforts to preserve India's craft tradition have been made, yet with the onslaught of 'modernization' and 'industrialization', life in the village is changing rapidly. Old, traditional, environmentally sound crafts are being replaced by the inherent vulgarity of mass-produced machine-made items and a plastic culture. However, shops, craft emporia and regular craft fairs are to be found in all major cities in India. Urban patronage via the fashion industry and an expanding export market has given some support to these crafts and the artists who preserve centuries-old skills and techniques.

FOOD AND DRINK

For centuries, the lure of India's spices, and the huge profits to be made from them, drew traders to the subcontinent. Pepper, cinnamon, nutmeg, ginger, cardamom, turmeric, coriander and an infinite variety of other flavourings form the basis of all Indian cuisine, subtly enhancing the taste of food and characterizing regional dishes.

It may come as a surprise to foreign visitors to discover that 'curry', certainly as it is known in the West, is unknown in India. Indian cooks create the flavour by blending freshly ground spices, and curry powder has no place in the culinary repertoire.

Local cooking varies throughout the country but, in general, considerably more meat, in particular chicken or lamb, is eaten in the north where, historically, the influences of Central Asia and the Middle East have had the greatest impact. Here, the *tandoor* or clay oven is traditionally used to bake food that has first been marinated with herbs and yoghurt. Breads, such as *naan*, are also baked in these ovens. Vegetarian dishes predominate in the south, invariably served with rice. The surrounding waters of the southern peninsula provide a harvest of fish and other seafoods such as crabs, lobsters and prawns.

Indian sweetmeats, usually very sweet indeed, are widely available. Often milk-based, they may be flavoured with almonds, rosewater, coconut or sweet spices. *Kulfi*, a rich ice-cream with pistachio nuts, is universally popular, as are *gulub jamuns* – fried sponge balls made with thickened milk and ground almonds and dipped in sugar syrup.

Fresh fruit is plentiful in India. It ranges from apples, pears and apricots in the north-west to a more tropical selection further south, where mangoes, bananas, watermelons and tangerines can be enjoyed in season.

India is famous for its fine teas, grown in the vast plantations of Darjeeling and Assam. Tea drinking is far more popular in the north than in the south, where coffee is the favourite beverage. Alcoholic drinks are subject to prohibition laws in certain states, notably in Gujarat, but beers and spirits are generally obtainable nearly everywhere else. Locally produced liquors such as toddy, or palm wine should be imbibed with caution.

Eating out can mean anything from experiencing world-class cuisine in international hotels to purchasing snacks from roadside vendors, but the true taste of India is found in private homes. Many housewives have spent a lifetime perfecting their culinary skills, and think little of taking an entire day to prepare dishes to suit exacting palates.

STATES, CITIES AND SITES

Each region of India has its own distinct character. The following gazetteer, covering all the Indian states and territories from north to south, gives a glimpse of the rich diversity .

The sheer variety of fabrics, dress and decorations in every part of the country and society is quite dazzling. In Rajasthan, women wear traditional skirts, veils and jewels (above), and fabric shops offer an enormous range of colours and patterns, as here in Jodhpur's Sardar market (above right). In many areas, popular fabrics include tie-dye, silk brocade and mirror embroidery (right), while throughout India, the best saris are made from richly coloured cottons and silks (far right).

Spices, such as chillies, turmeric, cloves and cardamom, are traditionally freshly ground in a pestle and mortar. Other ingredients and flavourings are added to create the distinctive taste of chicken masala, an Indian dish now known the world over.

home of a mainly pastoral community, and the valleys are now being terraced and cultivated. There are fruit orchards along the slopes and in spring blossoms are everywhere. The beauty of the landscape is being gradually marred as 'progress' moves up the mountains of Himachal Pradesh, cutting forests and polluting the streams and rivers.

The region was for long ruled by local chieftains and tribal communities, chief among them Gurkha migrants from Nepal. Ranjit Singh, the ruler of the Punjab, annexed the area in the 18th century and later it fell to the British. The British loved Himachal and built their summer capital in Shimla where officers could retreat from the heat of the plains. The lovely hill stations of Kulu-Manali, Chamba and Dalhousie still attract hordes of tourists during the summer, when these regions are cool and pleasant. Dharamsala is a focal point for exiled Tibetans as the home of the Dalai Lama.

Jammu and Kashmir, in the Himalayan ranges, is one of the finest mountainous regions in India. The state has two capitals, Jammu in winter and, in summer, Srinagar situated 1,730 metres (5,675 feet) above sea level in the Vale of Kashmir.

There are four distinct geophysical regions. The Tibetan tract of Ladakh, Gilgit and Skardu is largely snow-desert country and in the remote area of Ladakh are beautiful Buddhist monasteries. Further down is the lush valley of Kashmir, the pine forests and mountainous foothills of the Himalayas and Sivalik hills and the submontane slopes and plains.

The Mauryan emperor, Ashok, introduced Buddhism to this region. It later came under the rule of the Kushans, followed by the Huns and powerful Hindu rulers, seeing an intermingling and blending of Buddhist and Hindu traditions. During the medieval period Kashmir fell to Muslim rulers and Akbar, the Mughal emperor, conquered the idyllic valley in 1586. Srinagar became the summer haven for later Mughals who created beautiful gardens, palaces and mosques.

During the British colonial period, Kashmir, with its borders adjacent to several sensitive countries, remained a problematic region and in the wake of Independence, when India and Pakistan were divided, the situation proved no less difficult, as in Kashmir a

Hindu ruled over a largely Muslim population. Finally, it was decided to place the state of Kashmir in India. In 1948, soon after Independence, Kashmir was invaded by Pakistani forces. The UN enforced a cease-fire and the state was divided into Indian and Pakistani territory, and still remains a matter of dispute between the two countries.

Kashmir has a rich tradition of cottage industries, including woollen textiles and carpets, papier-mâché and wood carving, that earn substantial foreign exchange. The valley is very fertile and famous for its saffron and opium crops and harvest of walnuts, apples, strawberries and other exotic fruit. Most of the region's wealth, especially in Srinagar, Gulmarg and Sonamarg, was derived from the tourist industry that once poured visitors into the state during the summer seasons. The houseboats on the Dal Lake, the picturesque landscape and the opportunity to trek and ski in the Himalayas brought regular tourist traffic from all corners of the world.

Himachal Pradesh is one of the loveliest Himalayan states. As the name implies, it is the land of snow, and part of the landscape is dominated by mountains. Himachal is bounded by Jammu and Kashmir on the north, Punjab to the west, and Haryana to the south, while Tibet and Uttar Pradesh lie on its eastern borders. The mountain slopes are the

Punjab is bounded on the west by Pakistan, while to the north lies Jammu and Kashmir, and to the east and south are Himachal Pradesh, Haryana and Rajasthan. The state is located at the very mouth of the passageway from the west into the Gangetic plain.

Punjab has had a turbulent history which has seen the rise and fall of the Mauryan, Greek, Kushan and Gupta empires. When invasions brought Islamic rulers to the land, almost at the outset it was Punjab that they conquered. The Sikh religion took its roots here and its gurus and leaders broke away from the Mughals to unite and form a kingdom under the leadership of Ranjit Singh. After two Anglo-Sikh battles Punjab fell to the British in 1849. The British put in a lot of time and effort developing this region, establishing railways and cantonment cities, as Punjab was crucial to their operations.

Today Punjab, the land of the five rivers as it is aptly called, is a wealthy agricultural state, growing wheat, rice, pulses and several cash crops. With its vast irrigation projects, generous application of fertilizers and mechanization, this state provides surplus grain for the rest of the country. Industry is still in its nascent stage, but the woollen garment factories have been very successful in both Indian and foreign markets. Chandigarh is the capital of both Punjab and the neighbouring state of Haryana.

Haryana state was created in 1966. Its distant past still continues to be uncovered as archaeological excavations proceed, but for the most part it has been an ancillary to Delhi with a shared history. During British rule, Haryana was handed over to local powers and became a part of Punjab state.

Haryana's geography is interesting, with half the state lying in the sub-Himalayan *terai*, or grasslands, and the rest forming part of the Indo-Gangetic plains. The land is fertile and watered by the Ghaggar river, which is reason enough for Haryana to remain an essentially agricultural state. Haryana also has several industries that produce tractors, bicycles and sanitaryware. Panipat is its textile centre where cotton fabrics and carpets are produced.

Chandigarh is the shared capital of both Haryana and Punjab, and this has been a bone of contention for several years. The celebrated French architect Le Corbusier designed the city in the 1950s on a grand scale. It lacks any ancient buildings which usually grace the Indian landscape and is somewhat soulless, dominated by fading cement structures. For local Indian and foreign tourists, the state has created a number of tourist centres around lakes and parks that add a little charm to the green monotony.

Delhi is the capital of India, and despite its extreme climate of hot summers and harsh winters it has been chosen as the capital of many empires. The first city was built on the Yamuna, a major navigable river of north India and tributary of the Ganga. The river protects one side of the city while the Aravalli hills form a barrier on the other side.

The area is said to have been inhabited from prehistoric times. It was inherited by the Mauryas and the Guptas, and at the end of the 12th century Delhi became the capital of the first Islamic sultanate in India. Fine palaces, forts and mosques were built here in the 13th century. Later it became the capital of the Slave dynasty, the Khaljis and Tughluqs, Lodis and the Mughals, each new dynasty abandoning the Delhi of the previous dynasty and building their own new capital. Delhi is heir to the remains of seven medieval

capitals spread over its 1,483 square kilometre (572 square mile) expanse.

In 1911, Delhi was declared the capital of the British Empire in India. Once again a new site was chosen and two architects were assigned the task of designing the city of New Delhi. They used imperial designs from around the world, the result being a cultural cocktail of imposing administrative buildings, gardens, residential houses, broad streets and processional roads.

In 1947, when Independence was declared, New Delhi was retained as the capital and vast resources were invested in maintaining it as a showpiece of modern India. The

Whether school is reached by foot, car or cart (as here in Delhi), India is proud of a growing literacy rate and more chances of education.

city is now one of the largest commercial centres of northern India. The surrounding villages are being gradually whittled away by burgeoning small-scale industries, and factories have mushroomed everywhere. The wealthy Delhi-ites with their exponentially increasing numbers of cars and scooters have inevitably added to the pollution, as in any great city, but Delhi is still a wonderful introduction to India because the capital has so

much to offer: beautiful museums, medieval forts and palaces, first-rate hotels, fabulous shops and a lively contemporary arts scene.

Rajasthan, as the name suggests, is the land of the kings or rajas. This alluring state, situated in the north-west, is one of the largest in the country. Part of the land is arid desert and some of the most romantic medieval forts and palaces have been built here.

This region, one of the many gateways to the Gangetic plains, has been the traditional home of the Rajputs, a martial community known for their valour and courage and extraordinarily good looks. The Rajput clans are divided into branches, many of which rose to power some time in history. Prominent among them are the Mewars of Udaipur with their original fort at Chittor, the royal family of Jaipur, the Marwars of Jodhpur and clans from Bundi, Kota and Alwar. Other branches spread to central India and dominated the local political scene. Still to be seen are the wonderful palaces and forts of Jaisalmer, Bikaner, Bundi, Jodhpur and the capital, Jaipur.

The state produces cereals and pulses for local consumption and there are few industries to mar the landscape. Rajasthan evokes the sounds of lilting desert music, visions of decorative desert village houses, roads where camels still amble along, and where the many-hued clothes worn by the inhabitants present a striking contrast to the softer colours of the sands.

Uttar Pradesh is the most populous Indian state. It was also one of the largest states until November 2000 when the northern part of the state, embracing the foothills of the Himalaya, became the new state of **Uttaranchal**, with Dehra Dun as its capital. These two states encompass geophysical areas of enormous diversity. To the north are the foothills of the Himalayas, the *terai*, valleys and grasslands and here are the lovely Corbett and Dudhwa National Parks. To the south are the hill plateaux, and in the centre the wide sweep of the Gangetic valley. This valley is most densely populated with cele-

Delhi Road, the main street of Jaipur, state capital of Rajasthan, is famous for its decorated house façades, where 'Jaipur pink' is relieved by white fretted window screens and white-painted columns and panels.

brated cities built on the banks of the Ganga: Rishikesh and Haridwar marking the place where the river reaches the plains; Allahabad, the meeting place of the Ganga and its great tributary the Yamuna; and Varanasi, the most sacred Hindu pilgrimage centre in the world. Once the capital of India, Agra, with its Taj Mahal and Mughal forts, graces the higher reaches of the Yamuna.

Lucknow, the capital, is a celebrated cultural centre; the region has produced many artists, poets and philosophers. The state is also famous for its cottage industries: the carpets of Mirzapur, the inlay-work of Agra, the embroidery of Lucknow, the terracotta of Gorakpur and the woodwork of Saharanpur.

Uttar Pradesh is the country's largest producer of foodgrains, sugar-cane and oilseeds. A colossal network of railways, roads and airports spreads throughout the entire region. This state has a powerful presence in the Indian parliament and as the representative of the heartland of Hindi-speaking people it commands enormous political influence.

Madhya Pradesh was once the largest state in India, but in November 2000 the new state of **Chattisgarh** was carved out of its eastern region, with Raipur as its capital. The name Chattisgarh means 'thirty-six fortresses', referring to the several princely states in this region. These two states lie in the centre of the subcontinent. The region

was inhabited from earliest times, as is evident from the Stone Age sites near Bhopal, the capital city. The area became an important part of the Mauryan kingdom in the 2nd century BC and there is a famous Buddhist site at Sanchi.

The earliest Hindu temples were built here in the Gupta era (5th century) at Deogarh and Sanchi. Later, as provincial empires grew, other areas were developed. Magnificent temples, adorned with erotic sculptures, appeared in Khajuraho, the seat of power of the Chandella rulers in the 10th and 11th centuries. Great fortified palaces were built at Gwalior, Mandu and Chanderi. Later, Madhya Pradesh became part of the Mughal empire. The Marathas came to power in the 18th and 19th centuries, to be replaced by local rulers who struggled under British pressure to cede territory.

Madhya Pradesh is mainly an agricultural state with large tracts of forest land preserved in the Kanha, Panna, Bandhavgarh and Sanjay National Parks.

The cottage industries and handloom textiles of Chanderi and Maheshwari, famous in bygone days, have recently been revived. There are large steel plants, automobile and heavy electrical factories spread throughout the region, making Madhya Pradesh the seventh most industrialized state in India.

The state of Chattisgarh has a sizeable tribal population that still inhabits these fast-diminishing forests, and their culture and lifestyle are always under threat of exploitation.

Bihar has also been divided into two separate entities. On the eastern boundary of Bihar lies West Bengal, to the south lies **Jharkhand**, and on its northern border lies the Himalayan kingdom of Nepal. The capital of Bihar is Patna. The new state of Jharkhand has Madhya Pradesh to the west and West Bengal on the eastern border.

The new state of Jharkhand has inherited vast mineral and coal deposits, making it potentially one of the wealthiest states of India. However, this new state is backward in many areas, and until infrastructural development takes place, this area is locked in the medieval period with feudal lords who still reign supreme over a population yet to experience democracy.

Historically, Bihar has been one of the most significant states of India. Two thou-

sand five hundred years ago, the Buddha came to Gaya in Bihar to meditate, and it was here that he received his enlightenment or *Nirvana*. The town of Bodh Gaya still celebrates the Buddha's great spiritual awakening and is visited by thousands of Buddhists from around the world. Other important Buddhist sites in Bihar included Nalanda, the ancient university that brought students from distant lands like China, and the historic cities of Rajgir and Vaishali.

The present capital, Patna, is believed to have been the location of the ancient capital of Pataliputra of the Mauryas and Guptas between the 2nd century BC and the 5th century AD. Patna has a museum with a fine collection that traces the history of this region for over 3,000 years.

The principal agricultural produce of the state is rice, followed by wheat and maize, while the main cash crops are sugar-cane, potatoes, tobacco and jute. Jharkhand's wealth now lies in its huge mining projects, steel plants in Bokara and Jamshedpur, copper at Ghatsila, and coal and fertilizer factories in other areas.

Orissa is situated in the north-east of the peninsula, facing the Bay of Bengal in the east, and surrounded by its neighbours Jharkhand and Chattisgarh, West Bengal and Andhra

The Residency in Lucknow, the state capital of Uttar Pradesh, was the scene of the Siege of Lucknow during the Indian Uprising or Mutiny of 1857. It has been preserved exactly as it was when relieved.

Pradesh. It is a land of great natural beauty, with beaches at Puri and Gopalpur, great forests such as the Similipal National Park and Tiger Reserve and Chilka, the famous lake where migratory birds from all over the world flock in the winter months.

The state was known in ancient times as Kalinga, a kingdom of great wealth with trading contacts extending to the Far East, Indonesia and China. In the 2nd century BC the Mauryan emperor, Ashok, after a long and terrible battle at Kalinga, converted to the peaceful path of Buddhism. The site of his conversion is marked by an Ashokan inscription and a 20th-century monument called the Peace *stupa*.

It was during the rule of the Gangas that this region came into its own and great cultural activity changed the land. Beautiful temples were built, over a hundred in the vicinity of Bhubaneshwar. At Konarak the stone chariot temple was dedicated to the sun god, and in Puri the temple to Jagannath, Lord of the Universe. This temple is still used for worship and is the centre of the *Rath Yatra*, the great procession in which thousands of devotees pull the chariots of the gods through the streets. The state has sizeable Jain, Muslim and Christian poulations, and many other religious edifices of interest. Orissa has an ancient tradition of literature, music, dance, theatre and puppetry. The crafts and textiles of this region are unique to it, and a visit here can prove very rewarding.

Rice fields are the most common sight in the villages of Orissa and more than 80 per cent of the population work on the fields. Today the rural landscape is slowly changing as small-scale industries mushroom.

West Bengal is one of the leading cultural states of eastern India. Its southern shores are washed by the Bay of Bengal, to the north the boundaries meet Sikkim, Bhutan and Nepal, and it lies between Bihar on the west and Bangladesh to the east.

The juxtaposition of this area at the delta region of the Ganga added to its importance in historical times. In the medieval period the Palas, followed by the Sena rulers, created a powerful kingdom in Bengal, establishing its creative genius for centuries to come. Bengal was captured by Akbar in 1576 and controlled by various Mughal governors.

In 1690, an Englishman, Job Charnock,

In Orissa, Puri's main street, Grand Road, is frequently filled with visitors, who come to visit both the temple of Jagannath, one of the most holy pilgrimage places for Hindus, and its long sandy beach on the Bay of Bengal.

selected three villages that formed the basis of the city that is now called Kolkota. After 1757, the outcome of the Battle of Plassey (now Palashi) changed the history of Bengal. British interests in the region grew enormously, and Kolkota soon became the London of the East with fine buildings and churches built for the expanding British population living there. Today Kolkota is one of the most densely populated cities in India, foremost in literary and artistic activities, with a strong tradition of progressive theatre and cinema. Pressure on land has created slums of incredible poverty and a vast mobile population that migrates from the rural areas to the city.

Agriculture, especially rice cultivation, is the focus of life in Bengal. Much land is under cultivation and with the development of irrigation networks, the state is trying to release itself from depending on the vagaries of the monsoons. Industrial growth has been slow but there are factories producing automobiles, chemicals, ceramics, jute and paper.

Sikkim is a mountain state that lies east of Nepal, south of Tibet and west of Bhutan. It is through Sikkim that one finds the shortest route to Tibet, a journey that many pilgrims have taken through the centuries.

Sikkim, an independent kingdom until 1975, has an ancient tradition and was ruled by the Namgyal dynasty from the 17th century. Buddhism is still practised here and there are several important centres such as Gangtok, the capital, Yuksam, the meeting place of the three great Lamas, and the monasteries of Dubdi and Rumtek, poised on peaceful hilltops and surrounded by forests. The state is still largely forested, with a wide variety of plant species, including orchids, rhododendrons and magnolias. The mountains are very dramatic, often rising from the green foothills to 7,000 metres (23,000 feet) or more. Kanchenjunga, the world's third highest peak, is best seen in the early morning, before clouds hide the stunning view.

Assam is a beautiful and picturesque state and essentially constitutes the river basin of the Brahmaputra river which runs through it like a central vein. This gigantic river is over 5 kilometres (3 miles) wide during the floods and on both sides stretch vast flat alluvial plains. Assam is bounded by Arunachal Pradesh and Bhutan in the north, Nagaland to the east and Manipur and Mizoram to the south. To the south-west Assam touches the borders of Bangladesh and West Bengal.

This riverine area has a very ancient history and a unique cultural heritage that blends the fortunes of both India and Myanmar (Burma). The Ahom dynasty held sway in the

Throughout India, traditional and modern modes of transport co-exist in a wide variety of forms. Bullock carts piled high with thorn bushes for fuel (above left) and elephants laden with long grasses (above right) are as familiar a sight in rural areas as the ubiquitous rickshaws, *powered by foot, pedal or motor (opposite, bottom left), are in every town and city. Water buses (opposite, top left) ply canals and backwaters, while the Indian Railways network (opposite, right) crisscrosses the country.*

region and ruled from the 13th to the 19th century. Their culture and patronage saw a great flowering of music, dance, temple building and literature in Assam. There is also a very old and beautiful tradition of weaving raw silk and cotton textiles, and a fine bamboo cottage industry.

While agriculture is the main occupation, during the British Raj large tracts of land were stripped of their virgin forests and converted into tea plantations. Today, Assam produces about 15 per cent of the world's tea. Small areas of the original forest landscape are now being preserved in the northern Kaziranga National Park and on the Bhutan border at the Manas National Park.

The capital of Assam state is Guwahati, which stands on the south bank of the Brahmaputra. Perched on a hill beside the river is the famous old temple of Kamakhya, overlooking the great expanse of water, where animal sacrifices are still performed to appease the great goddess of fertility.

Meghalaya formed part of Assam for several years after Independence. In 1970, this pretty hilly region, called 'the abode of the clouds',

became a state. It has Assam as its neighbour on the northern side and Bangladesh on the southern boundary.

The Khasi and the Jainta Hills form an imposing stretch of scenery running across central and eastern Meghalaya. A number of non-navigable rivers pour down from the hillsides, giving the landscape an extremely picturesque appearance and resulting in great fertility. Though agriculture is the principal occupation, the terrain prevents large-scale farming and the fields and terraces on the slopes tend to be small.

Much of the land is under forest and Meghalaya has its share of remarkably rare species of animal and plant life. The exotic insect-eating pitcher plant is found in the region of the south Garo and west Khasi hills. The forest also provides commercial wood like teak, bamboo and cane.

The capital of Meghalaya is Shillong, which is a popular base for tourists visiting the delightful trekking areas and scenic spots of the region. While schools, hospitals and industries are needed to improve the standard of living of the people, some efforts have to be made to ensure that Meghalaya maintains its

natural and cultural heritage.

Arunachal Pradesh, 'land of the rising sun', is situated on the easternmost tip of India, with Bhutan to the west, Tibet and China to the north, Myanmar (Burma) to the east and Assam to the south. It is a mountainous state, covered with lush bamboo groves, evergreen tropical forests and grasslands that provide superb wildlife habitats. The mighty Brahmaputra river that rises in Tibet sweeps through the Himalayas in a wide curve in Arunachal Pradesh, then flows through Assam and into Bangladesh, where it drains into the Bay of Bengal. Only 4 per cent of the land in Arunachal Pradesh is under cultivation, 62 per cent is forested.

There are only 12 towns in Arunachal, and Itanagar is the state capital, where one can see the historic fort of Ita. There are beautiful Buddhist monasteries, like Bomdila and Tawang. Permits are needed for travel in this border state, as they are in many other of the north-eastern hill states.

Nagaland is surrounded by Arunachal Pradesh in the north, Assam to the west,

Manipur in the south, with Myanmar (Burma) to the east, but the proximity of this state to so many others in the north-east region of India has not hindered the growth of a unique cultural identity. Several distinct tribal groups inhabit this land, and have done so for centuries. They are a colourful people and each tribe is identifiable by its unique ceremonial dress, headgear and jewellery.

During the 12th and 13th centuries Nagaland formed part of the Ahom kingdom, with its nucleus in the present-day state of Assam. During the British period it was brought under foreign rule. Missionaries worked in this region, converting large numbers to Christianity and severely affecting the cultural fabric of the people.

With government incentives, agriculture has become the main occupation of the people, with rice as the basic food crop. Industrial growth has remained slow and many villages do not have electricity. Kohima is the capital but Dimapur is the only town within Nagaland where rail and air services are available, linking it to other states.

Manipur faces Myanmar (Burma) along its east and southern boundary, while its north, west and southern sides adjoin the easternmost Indian states of Nagaland, Assam and Mizoram. The state is divided into two geographical zones: the hilly areas and the plains. The plains are slowly being cultivated with rice fields which provide the staple diet of the area. The hilly forests are some of the finest in India, with rare orchids, trees and plants. The state is also the home of the extremely rare Brow-antlered Deer.

The history of the state is one of great trials and tribulations. Very powerful local kings ruled this region. Buddhism and, later, Hinduism penetrated the area and soon led to the flowering of unique forms of music, dance and theatre. The local rulers were forced into battle with the neighbouring Burmese and the Chinese who they defeated several times in the course of history. In 1762 the Manipuri king made a treaty with the British to ward off the Burmese offensive. This resulted in the British keeping Manipur as a native state. After Independence, Manipur, along with other sensitive areas in the north-eastern region, was given the protected status of a union territory. In 1972, Manipur was made a fully fledged state of the Indian republic. Imphal, the fast-growing capital, has its own university, the state museum and an academy of dance where the famous *Manipuri* dances are performed.

Mizoram, sandwiched between Bangladesh on the west and Myanmar (Burma) to the east, formed part of Assam until 1970. After first being given the status of a union territory, it became the 23rd Indian state in 1987. It is a land of great beauty, with hill ranges running north to south, some over 900 metres (3,000 feet) high. The highest peak in the region, Phawngpui, the Blue Mountain, rises to 2,210 metres (7,250 feet).

The principal occupation is agriculture, with *jhum* cultivation and terrace farming. Orchards, and fruit-canning and juice-making factories are being set up to industrialize the area. Still quite inaccessible, Mizoram is linked by road and air from its capital in Aizawl. This city has become the cultural centre of the state, with shops selling local textiles and handicrafts which stem from a long and ancient tradition.

More than any other city in India, Mumbai, the capital of Maharashtra state, has embraced the Westernized world market as a centre of finance, films and commerce. Not far from the skyscrapers, however, fishermen with dug-out canoes still pursue a traditional lifestyle.

Tripura state is bordered on three sides by Bangladesh, one of the anomalies of Partition in 1947, and forms part of the great river valley of Bangladesh. It is largely an agricultural state and has not yet suffered the impact of industrialization.

The area's history is recorded in Bengali poetry. The kings of Tripura held their own, but suffered under the impact of the Mughal army, and in addition had to ward off threats from neighbouring kings of West Bengal. In later years the Maharaja Birchandra Manikya Bahadur, ruler of Tripura, made valiant efforts to reform the administrative structure of his kingdom, using the British style of administration as his model. After Independence, Tripura fell into the Indian union and with democracy came the end of monarchy and its accompanying glamour and romance. Agartala, the state capital, is mainly a commercial centre, its chief building of interest being the vast Ujjayanta Palace.

Gujarat is one of the largest states in western India. To the west and north are Pakistan, and the Indian state of Rajasthan, and to the east and south are the states of Madhya Pradesh and Maharashtra.

Historically, Gujarat is one of the oldest regions of habitation in India. At Lothal, excavations have revealed remains of the Indus Valley Civilization with its urban complex dating back 5,000 years. This region, with its ports and coastland facing the Arabian Sea, was important for trade with western countries throughout history.

Porbandar in Gujarat is the birthplace of Mahatma Gandhi, who spearheaded the national freedom movement. The town and the ashrams built by Gandhi attract many visitors who come to understand how Gandhi's philosophy of non-violence and peaceful coexistence is practised.

Gujarat has rich black soil ideal for growing tobacco, and has from ancient times been famous for its cotton. Much of the land in the north is dry and is used for growing cash crops such as ground-nuts. A powerful industrial community is centred in the manufacture of textiles, chemicals, petrochemicals and pharmaceuticals, and there are hundreds of other small-scale enterprises.

There are over 40 ports in Gujarat, with Kandla as the most important. Cities like Ahmedabad, Gandhinagar the capital, Vadodara (Gujarat's university and cultural centre), historic sites at Lothal and the temples of Dwarka and Modhera are fascinating places to visit. The National Park and Lion Reserve at Gir, and the Wild Ass Sanctuary in the Kuchchh area make Gujarat a wonderful and as yet undiscovered state to explore.

Daman and Diu is a small union territory measuring only 112 square kilometres (43 square miles). This area was colonized along with Goa by the Portuguese and was integrated into India in 1961. Daman lies 193 kilometres (120 miles) north of Mumbai on the coast of the southern edge of Gujarat, just north of Dadra and Nagar Haveli.

The little island of Diu lies off the coast of Gujarat on the Gulf of Cambay and is connected to the mainland by two bridges. Diu has the same characteristics as the Junagadh district of Gujarat that it adjoins, and the land is dry. The government is making efforts to develop agriculture and industries here.

Dadra and Nagar Haveli is a small union territory of 491 square kilometres (190 square miles) which forms a pocket between Gujarat and Maharashtra. It has a curious history. The Marathas gave rights to collect revenue from the villages of this region to the Portuguese in 1779 in return for their cooperation. The Portuguese ruled the area until 1954 when the local people declared independence. Dadra and Nagar Haveli, consisting of some 72 villages, was merged with the Indian union in 1961 when it was given the special status of a union territory.

Over 79 per cent of the population is tribal and engaged in the cultivation of rice and other minor cereals. The forest areas of Dadra and Nagar Haveli provide the tribals with crucial supplementary income. There are road links to 67 villages and railway lines run to Vapi from Mumbai and Ahmedabad. The capital, Silvassa, is 18 kilometres (11 miles) from Vapi, the nearest railhead.

Maharashtra is one of the largest states on the west coast of peninsular India. Like Gujarat, it has large farms for the cultivation of cotton, groundnut, oil-seeds and some of the finest varieties of mango in India.

Sharing its inland boundary with Madhya Pradesh, the state has played an important role in Indian history. It was part of the Satavahana kingdom and important Buddhist sites, where fabulous cave temples were hollowed out of the rock, developed in Karle, Kanheri (outside Mumbai, the capital), Ajanta and Ellora in the Aurangabad district. The land is dotted with forts, many of which were built by Shivaji, the great 17th-century Maratha warrior, to withstand Islamic forces.

44

In 1534, the local nawab gave the islands of Mumbai to the Portuguese in exchange for assistance against the Mughal rulers. In 1662, when Charles II of England married Catherine of Braganza, Britain was given the islands as part of the royal dowry. The British Crown rented out the islands to the East India Company for £10 per annum. In the days of the East India Company, Mumbai and its harbour were developed and the local Parsi community and other businessmen contributed to its vast ship-building activities.

Today, Mumbai is India's most important commercial centre. Built on seven islands linked by bridges, with skyscrapers and flyovers, it is like Hong Kong, and there is no other Indian city like it. Some attractive Victorian buildings remain, and the huge arch known as the Gateway of India stands as a monument to the colonial past. India produces more films per year than any other country in the world and much of the action is staged here in Mumbai's Bollywood.

Karnataka state lies on the west coast of India, just south of Goa. Its 300-kilometre (186-mile) long beach faces the Arabian Sea. Behind this narrow, but beautiful and unspoilt coastal strip is the wall formed by the Western Ghats. This rugged region, once covered with thick tropical vegetation, moves on to blend with the southern part of the Deccan plateau. A large part of Karnataka lies on this plateau, much of which is dry because it falls within the rainshadow of the Ghats. The state is drained by five rivers: the Godavari, Krishna, Kaveri, Palar and Pennar.

Karnataka has had a very diverse past, with evidence of human habitation from the Stone Age. The advent of the Chalukyas with their capital in Badami and the temples of Aihole and Pattadkal gave to the region a great artistic tradition. In the 14th century, the Vijayanagara empire grew around its capital near Hampi and offered a challenge to all southern states and the sultans of Delhi. The magnificent remains at Vijayanagara can be seen in a complex of forts, palaces and temples standing beside the Tungabhadra river.

The Islamic period heralded great architectural achievement in Bijapur, Bidar and Gulbarga by the Bahamani sultans. The 18th century brought to a head the rivalry between Hyder Ali's family and the British, and with the slaying of Tipu Sultan the British troops stormed and captured the fort of Srirangapatnam. The forts and palaces of Tipu in the area of Mysore echo some of the flavour of those valiant days.

Mysore became the seat of royal power and Bangalore the paradigm of British country living. Bangalore, with its pleasant climate, was once called the garden city, but today it is the electronic city of India and one of the fastest-growing in Asia.

Though largely an agricultural state growing rice, other cereals and pulses, Karnataka also has large tea and coffee estates in the district of Kodagu. The area of Mysore is famous for silk cultivation and its sandalwood cottage industry. Industrial development in the state has been exceptional, with public sector undertakings such as electronics, aeronautics, fertilizers and chemicals. Steel plants and gold mining in the region have added to its wealth and prosperity.

Goa is one of India's smallest states and also one of the most idyllic, with lovely beaches washed by the Arabian Sea, an undulating landscape and lush vegetation. Situated on the west coast of the Indian peninsula, Goa is bounded on the north by the state of Maharashtra and to the south by Karnataka.

The region has had a very interesting and chequered history. In the early centuries of the Christian era, it fell under the rulers of the Deccan. Subsequently it was occupied by the sultans of Bijapur. After Vasco da Gama discovered the sea route to India via the Cape of Good Hope off South Africa, Portuguese ships and traders began to come to the west coast of India. In 1510 Afonso da Albuqerque captured Goa from the Sultan of Bijapur after a fierce battle, commemorating his victory on St Catherine's Day by building a church to this saint. This was the beginning of a long rule by the Portuguese in Goa. They built forts to protect their coast and these monuments, like Aguada, Terekhol, Chapora and Cabo de Rama, still stand staring out at the deep blue of the Arabian Sea. The Portuguese capital, now called Old Goa, became the centre of Christianity and enormous churches, monasteries and convents were established here. A few of the old buildings remain on the largely ruined site. In 1542 the Jesuit priest Francis Xavier came to India and made many converts. His body still lies in state in the church of Bom Jesus. On 16 December 1961, 14 years after the rest of India had attained Indepen-dence, Goa was liberated from Portuguese rule after almost 450 years, and became a state in 1987.

Goa has a very luxuriant landscape and everything appears to grow there. There are coconut, cashew nut and betel nut planta-

Karnataka's complex history generated a rich architectural heritage in the form of many temples, including the Hoysala examples at Somnathpur, Belur and Halebid. Begun in the 12th century, the latter was never completed, though its superb carvings, archetypal columns and vast Nandi, the god Shiva's bull, make it the finest of the Hoysala temples.

tions. Rice is the major crop and forms part of the staple diet of the Goans. Fishing boats, large and small, operate all along the coastal area.

Since it is well linked by air, road and rail, thousands of visitors come to Goa each year to enjoy Goan hospitality, to visit Panaji, the capital, to see the churches of Old Goa and the forts, and to bathe from the quiet peaceful beaches during the cool winter months.

Andhra Pradesh is situated in the Deccan, south of the Vindhya range, its eastern side facing the Bay of Bengal, the rest of the region bounded by Orissa, Chattisgarh, Maharashtra, Karnataka and Tamil Nadu. The state's geographical position has contributed to a shared historical identity with several neighbours. There are remains of prehistoric habitations and evidence of prosperous Buddhist settlements by the 2nd century BC in Amaravati and Nagarjunakonda.

More than 70 per cent of the population is engaged in agriculture. The principal crops are rice, other cereals and pulses, and Andhra Pradesh produces more than 94 per cent of India's total virginia tobacco crop. Industrial growth has transformed the landscape, for Andhra is very rich in mineral wealth with copper, manganese, mica and coal mines. The state is efficiently run with a wide network of roads, rail links and airports. The major seaport on the east coast facing the Bay of Bengal is Vishakhapatnam.

The capital of the state is the medieval city of Hyderabad. The Qutub Shahi rulers of the 16th century established themselves in Golconda, which played a very important role in south Indian politics, and built a magnificent fort a few kilometres outside Hyderabad. The Nizams who ruled from Hyderabad accumulated fabulous wealth, much of it in the form of gemstones. In 1953 when the state was being reconstituted the area took its present shape and form. Hyderabad has some fine palaces that once belonged to the Nizam and his nobles, and the famous royal collection of antiques, miniature paintings, textiles and jewellery is displayed in the Salar Jung Museum.

Thousands of Indian pilgrims from every

The Dravidian temples of Tamil Nadu feature vast, soaring gopurams (gateways), covered in a profusion of coloured, sculpted figures. In Madurai, the Shree Meenakshi temple gopurams dominate the city's old centre.

corner of the country flock to Tirupati, one of India's most important temple sites. The Venkateshwara Temple, dedicated to Vishnu, is considered one of the wealthiest in India. It is said that the annual turnover from donations amounts to billions of rupees. With its

While Kerala's tropical sunshine is much enjoyed by visitors, the local traffic police protect themselves with parasols.

wealth the temple has set up a university and several hospitals and schools.

Kerala forms the south-western tip of India. The state has a long coastline on the Arabian Sea, over which the early traders from the Middle East came to India bringing Jews and Christians to its shores. The Jewish and Christian communities built settlements and religious buildings, greatly influencing the cultural development of the area. In the late 15th century Vasco da Gama landed in Kochi, an important port town of Kerala, and from here the Portuguese went further north along the coast to conquer Goa.

The coastal area receives both the southwest and winter monsoons, and its warm humid climate has created a fertile region where grass may be seen growing on tarmac roads and on the red-tiled sloping roofs of the houses. The coastland is covered with coconut palms which provide the people's basic requirements of oil, food, leaves with which to thatch their roofs and fibre for rope-making. Further inland, amid the undulating ghat regions, is the Silent Valley, one of the few surviving areas of rainforest, which Indian environmentalists fought hard to save. The rest of the area contains prosperous rubber, cashew, areca nut and spice plantations.

Kovalam, near the capital, Thiruvanathapuram, is the best of the known beaches. The port of Kochi offers views of early Jewish and Dutch homes, and an opportunity of sailing through the backwaters and peaceful canals. There are several wildlife parks in Kerala including Thekkadi on the banks of the Periyar river.

Tamil Nadu is one of the best places to experience the richness of south Indian culture, covering the entire spectrum from food, to temples, music, dance and rural pageantry. The state stands on the south-eastern side of the peninsula. At its southernmost point, Kanya Kumari, where the Arabian Sea, the Bay of Bengal and the Indian Ocean meet, thousands go to watch the glorious spectacle of sunset and moonrise on the same horizon.

The history of Tamil Nadu has been one of great achievements. From the Sangam era cultural activity of the most sophisticated kind was patronized here. Later, the powerful kingdoms of the Pallavas, Cheras, Cholas and Pandyas not only brought south Indian art and culture to great heights but carried it beyond the shores of India to the Far East. The British East India Company set up its fort in Chennai, now the state capital, in 1640 and thus began a very different cultural episode. Fine gothic churches, palatial administrative buildings, warehouses and ports sprang up along the coast.

The state has principally an agriculture-based economy with much of the land under rice cultivation. Cash crops such as sugar, oil-seeds and fruit are also grown. In the hilly regions of the ghats, amidst forests and around hill stations like Udagamandalam, large tea and coffee plantations prosper.

Industrial development in Tamil Nadu includes large-scale factories for the production of automobiles, bicycles, textiles, fertilizers, cement, steel, railway wagons and other ancillary items. The state is also an exporter of tanned leather goods, silk, the famous Chennai checked cotton, tea, coffee and granite. But it is for the resplendent temples, more than can be visited in months of travelling, that one goes to Tamil Nadu. No other state has such architecture to compare.

Puduchcheri is a union territory and comprises the former French-occupied areas of Puduchcheri, Karaikal, Mahé and Yanam. These tiny territories are dispersed at some distance from one another. The capital, which lends its name to the whole territory, lies on the east coast facing the Bay of Bengal encircled by the South Arcot district of Tamil Nadu. It is a lovely town with a discernible French flavour. The pretty beach-side strand is suggestive of Nice, with colonial homes and administrative buildings.

Karaikal lies 150 kilometres (93 miles) south of Puduchcheri and Mahé is situated on the west coast within the state of Kerala. Yanam is located further north on the east coast in the East Godavari district of Andhra Pradesh. Over 45 per cent of the population are engaged in agriculture and lush green rice fields are characteristic of the landscape.

The Lakshadweep islands are situated off the coast of Kerala in south-western India and comprise several groups, including the Laccadives, Minicoy and Amindivi. Some islands are tiny and uninhabited, others have beautiful beaches, and some are gradually being submerged by the sea.

These islands were originally inhabited by local tribes such as the Amini, Kalpeni, Andrott, Kavaratti and Aggatti. They were then converted to Islam by early settlers who

The Andaman Islands have only recently become part of the tourist itinerary. The clear waters around the islands, their coral reefs and sandy beaches make the Andamans a tropical paradise.

had trade links with Kerala. In the 16th century the Portuguese tried to conquer the islands to control the shores of Kerala and Goa. The inhabitants sought the help of Kerala and were saved from the Portuguese, only to fall under the rule of the Moplah ruler of Cannanore. They turned to Tipu Sultan of Mysore for aid but when Tipu's kingdom was captured by the British, the islands fell under the control of the East India Company.

Today the Lakshadweep islands are connected by sea routes and a helicopter service links the capital, Kavaratti, and important townships such as Agatti to the mainland. In the interests of conservation, Bangaram is the only island open to tourism. Income is mainly generated from coconut plantations and fishing. The horror of industry has not yet contaminated these lovely islands.

The Andaman and Nicobar Islands lie in the Bay of Bengal, 1,255 kilometres (780 miles) from Kolkota and 1,190 kilometres (740 miles) from Chennai, forming an arc in the sea from the tip of Myanmar (Burma) to the island of Sumatra in Indonesia.

The Great Andamans consist of five islands, and to the south are the Little Andamans. There are over 204 islets, prominent among them Ritchies' Archip-elago and the Labyrinth Islands. Further south, 121 kilometres (75 miles) from the Little Andamans, is the cluster of 19 islands known as the Nicobars, chief among them Great Nicobar, Nancowrie, Car Nicobar and Trinket.

The islands have been inhabited for centuries by indigenous tribes such as the Great Andamanese, the Onge, the Jarawa and the Sentinelese. From 1857 to 1942 they were used by the British, like Australia, as a penal colony for the settlement of life and long-term criminals. In 1942, Japanese forces occupied the territory but the British regained control in 1945. The islands now form a part of the union of India.

The Andamans and Nicobars have a unique natural heritage, with evergreen moist deciduous and swamp forests. The unspoilt areas have an abundance of bird and animal species, several of which are endemic to the islands. In recent years agricultural growth has seen the cultivation of rice, the principal food crop, along with coconut and areca nut as the main cash crops of the region. Fruit orchards for mango, banana, pineapple and papaya have also been added.

Today, towns such as Port Blair, the capital, in the south Andamans have grown and tourism is being developed to entice more people to enjoy the clean beaches and unpolluted waters that are already attracting divers and snorkellers. These lovely islands are accessible by sea and air, with flights operating out of Kolkota and Chennai to Port Blair, and ferries sailing from Kolkota, Chennai and Vishakhapatnam.

HIMALAYAN FOOTHILLS AND HILL STATIONS

NORTH-WESTERN INDIA

The greater part of north-western India is dominated by the mighty Himalayas, which create a natural barrier between Central Asia and the subcontinent. Melting snows from the mountains feed the river systems that pass through the foothills in Kashmir and the Himachal to irrigate the fertile wheat-producing valleys of Haryana and Punjab, and finally join with the Indus, Yamuna and Ganga rivers.

High in the mountains in India's most northerly state, Jammu and Kashmir, lies the isolated kingdom of Ladakh, its stark and barren 'moonscape' peppered with hilltop *gompas*, Tibetan Buddhist monasteries. Here, many of the *gompas* stage festivals, some arranged to coincide with the summer tourist season, where spectators join robed, shaven-headed lamas to watch pageants of musicians and masked dancers.

Summer is also the season in which to escape the heat of the plains and visit the relaxing hill stations, lush valleys and beautiful countryside of the Himalayan foothills, with their restorative temperate climate. The lovely Vale of Kashmir attracted the Mughals and, many centuries later, the British. The former created idyllic terraced gardens and palaces, and the latter built the comfortable houseboats that still line the banks of the Jhelum river and Dal and Nagin lakes in Srinagar, the state's summer capital. Outlying hill stations were the bases for walking, fishing and riding expeditions.

Today, the hill resorts of Himachal Pradesh are more popular starting points for such activities. Two of these, Kulu and Manali, lie at either end of the beautiful Kulu Valley, known as the apple orchard of India, famous for its spring blossom. Rural life here has changed little over many hundreds of years: men herd goats and sheep, and women spin and weave shawls and blankets in small villages. From here some of the best treks in India can be made, to the Parbati, Malana and Solang Valleys, or up across the Manali and other passes.

Many other hill resorts in Himachal Pradesh, such as Dharamsala, Dalhousie and Shimla, became fashionable in the British era. Dharamsala is now better known as the home of the exiled Dalai Lama and many of his Tibetan Buddhist followers. To the south-east lies Shimla, once the British summer capital and social hub of the Raj. Perched atop a spectacular ridge with far-reaching views on every side, its busy Mall, Gaiety Theatre and colonial hotels still thriving, its popularity as a resort continues unabated.

By contrast, Chandigarh, the capital of both Haryana and Punjab states, is a truly late-20th-century city, designed by the architect Le Corbusier and begun in 1952. The Punjab's largest city, Amritsar, lies far to the west, across the state's vast wheat fields. Its famous Golden Temple is the most sacred of all Sikh shrines.

Chief among the attractions of Srinagar, the Kashmiri summer capital, are two lakes: the massive Dal, near the city, and Nagin, 'the Jewel in the Ring', a smaller lake to the north bestrewn with carpets of beautiful water-lilies (opposite, top). *Many visitors stay on houseboats* (above), *originally built as summer residences by the British, who were not allowed to own land in Kashmir. They can be reached by water-taxis, or shikaras* (left), *which also serve as mobile shops.*

PREVIOUS PAGES
Page 48:*The remote Ladakh region lies high in the shadows of the Himalayas.* Page 49: *Traditional dress for many Ladakhi women means distinctive stove-pipe hats and brightly fringed shawls.*

Kashmir is famous for a huge range of crafts and produce, including carpets, painted papier mâché, wood carvings, saffron and honey; Srinagar's many markets are always crowded with women in their traditional Kashmiri headcloths (above). *In addition, the 'floating markets' on the lakes* (right) *sell fruit, vegetables and other provisions.*

The monasteries, or gompas, *that cling to the steep foothills of the Himalayas, such as that at Lamayuru* (opposite, centre right), *hold fast to traditional Tibetan Buddhist customs and teachings. Many* gompas *hold colourful festivals, for which the lamas dress in opulent silk robes and the local women wear turquoise-studded headdresses handed down over generations* (opposite, top right). *At the 15th-century Tikse* gompa, *in the Indus Valley south-east of Leh, the calm of regular lessons* (above) *gives way during festival time in late summer to a throng of lamas and visitors* (opposite, left). *Further down the valley, Hemis* gompa, *one of the largest monasteries in Ladakh, is famous for its extensive library and ancient scripts* (opposite, bottom right).

Left: *The Palace at Stok, near Leh, the Ladakh capital, has been the home of the Ladakhi royal family for over a century.*

Very little remains of Shey, the former Ladakhi capital; the royal palace, dating from the 15th century, was abandoned over 100 years ago and is today in a semi-ruined state. The small gompa *across the fields from the palace contains a massive 12m (39ft) statue of the Buddha* (far left), *the largest in Ladakh, constructed in the 17th century. During the harvest festival in August, a highly venerated monk* (above), *the 'living oracle', accompanied by his acolytes, dispenses advice and grants favours to supplicants* (left).

Far away to the west, across the wheat bowl of India, lies Amritsar, the largest city in Punjab, whose population is always swelled by devout Sikhs (above) *making their pilgrimage to the Golden Temple* (right). *The first temple complex was built by Arjun Dev, the fifth Sikh Guru, in the late 16th century. It was razed to the ground in 1761 but was rebuilt by the local community, gaining its name when Maharaja Ranjit Singh donated over 400kg (880lb) of gilded copper to roof the dome. Inside is the earliest extant copy of the* Guru Granth Sahib, *the holy book of the Sikhs, from which all other copies are made.*

Manali, in Himachal Pradesh, has been a hill resort frequented by Indians and foreigners alike for decades. In the 1970s it became a regular stop on the Hippie Trail, en route to the nearby village of Vashisht, but these days the majority of visitors come to enjoy the temperate climate and the town's delightful setting amidst beautiful countryside filled with orchards and blossoms. Manali is also a much-favoured base for skiing and walks, climbs and treks along the Beas river in the Kulu Valley to the south. The people in this part of the Himalayan foothills are very fair-skinned, particularly the women (above), and mostly live in small villages, such as Old Manali (left), where they continue to lead a rural lifestyle.

In the Kulu Valley south of Manali, life continues as it has for centuries, with sheep-
and goat-herding (right) still playing an important part in the rural economy of the
region. Of the many villages, each with its wooden temple, one of the least
outwardly affected by modern times is Nagar, on the terraced eastern slopes of
the Beas, across the river from Katrain, famous for its abundant fruit orchards.
Nagar was the regional capital until the mid-17th century, when the Rajas moved
to Kulu; they left behind the old stone-and-log Castle, now a hotel, and ancient
Hindu temples and shrines, some of which date back to the 11th century. The
archetypal Nagar house is constructed of wood, and most houses feature a
traditional balcony (above), positioned to give the best views of the lovely
surrounding countryside.

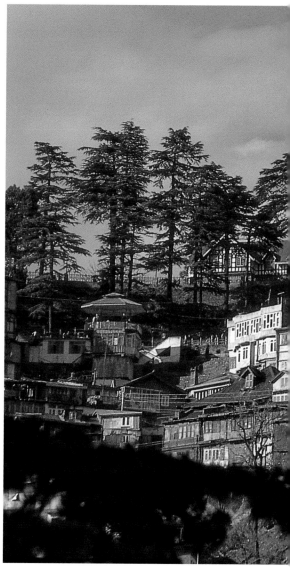

Manali is particularly well known for its weaving. The thick tweed-like cloth is used for clothing, blankets and shawls, as well as for the distinctive topis, *the embroidered 'pill-box' hats worn by the men of the Kulu Valley. The looms are often on the outside of houses in Old Manali, either against a ground-floor wall or on a balcony attached to the first storey (above left), which is reached by a ladder.*

West of Manali is Dharamsala, originally a British hill station and since 1960 the home in exile of the Dalai Lama and Tibetan government. The upper town, McLeodganj, is a 'Little Tibet', full of refugees, temples, schools, meditation centres and monasteries, outside which monks will gather for discussion and debate (left). Dharamsala is also the starting point for treks north to the mountainous Chamba Valley.

Shimla, in the Himalayan foothills, was 'discovered' by the British in 1817, when it was just a small village. Its commanding position on the crest of a ridge, cool air and lush countryside quickly made it a favourite summer resort. By 1864, when it was declared the summer seat of the government of India, the 'Queen of Hill Stations' had become the epitome of everything British. Today, it is a favourite Indian holiday resort, but it still retains a 19th-century British feel, with its church and half-timbered colonial houses on the ridge above the bazaar (above). The town is less than a day's train ride from Delhi, the last stage taken from Kalka on the famous narrow-gauge 'toy train' (right), which winds its way through spectacular scenery.

THE GOLDEN TRIANGLE AND THE PRINCELY STATES

FROM THE CAPITAL TO THE THAR DESERT

India's capital, Delhi, the first stop for many visitors to the country, is built on the foundations of at least seven former cities. The spacious 20th-century streets and broad avenues of the newest city, New Delhi, are in direct contrast to the bustling, narrow streets and bazaars of Old Delhi, which dates back to Mughal days; the whole metropolis is an extraordinary blend of the modern and ancient worlds.

Delhi is the most northerly point of the so-called 'golden triangle', the historic area most visited by tourists, that links three great cities – the other two being Agra and Jaipur. Agra, the south-eastern point, was once the capital of the Mughal empire, and is universally known for the exquisite Taj Mahal, the nearby Red Fort on the banks of the Yamuna river, and other magnificent examples of Mughal architecture.

To the west of Agra is the state of Rajasthan, home of the Rajput princes, whose proud history is remembered by innumerable astounding hill forts and grand palaces. Even the wildlife sanctuaries at Ranthambore, Bharatpur and Sariska are poignant reminders of the Rajputs' hunting expeditions and love of the chase. Much of Rajasthan is desert or semi-arid land, but there are fertile areas. Jaipur, the state capital, is known as the Pink City because of the colour in which its older buildings are painted, and reflects hundreds of years of history in the forts and palaces, such as Amber, Jaigarh and Nahagarh, that stand on the circle of hills that surround the city.

On the edge of the Thar Desert, Pushkar, set beside a peaceful lake, is the venue for the huge annual Camel Fair held in the autumn. Further west, magnificent hilltop forts rise above the sands: Jodhpur's Meherangarh Fort dominates the city below, and the great fort at Jaisalmer testifies to the town's importance as a major centre on the trade route from Central Asia. This is an ancient and romantic land, where the rolling dunes constantly change perspective in the ever-shifting light and colour flares out wherever people gather together in a multi-hued medley of bright turbans and vivid flowing veils.

In the south of Rajasthan, Udaipur is, by contrast, a green city of lakes and palaces. The quiet villages in the surrounding hills and valleys are disturbed only by pilgrims to such sites as the impressive Jain temples of Ranakpur and Mount Abu.

Evidence of the prosperity of the princes continues in Madhya Pradesh to the east; the hill fort at Gwalior was one of the most important strongholds in northern India during the medieval era, and at Orchha, south of Gwalior, an extensive complex of palaces and temples still overlooks the rich countryside. Near the state capital, Bhopal, one can visit the small village of Sanchi, one of the oldest and most important Buddhist sites in the subcontinent.

Old Delhi is a labyrinth of teeming streets filled with bazaars and historic buildings, many dating from the 17th century, when the city was called Shahjahanabad, after its Mughal creator. At the east end of Old Delhi's congested main street, Chadni Chowk, stands Shah Jahan's Red Fort (above), which, with its halls, palaces, gardens and mosques, is one of India's most superb memorials of the Mughal era. Further along Chadni Chowk can be found one of Old Delhi's impressive temples, the Gurudwara Sisganj Sikh temple (left).

PREVIOUS PAGES
Page 60: Pushkar's lake is reached by ghats, broad flights of steps, that run down to the sacred water; here, women descend bearing floral offerings and coconuts. Page 61: Chillis spread out to dry suffuse the Rajasthani landscape with a red glow.

South of Chadni Chowk is India's largest mosque, the Jama Masjid, built by Shah Jahan. Each of its entrances (right) opens onto a panorama of red sandstone and white marble, a combination of materials made famous by the great projects of the Mughal emperor-builders. The courtyard inside will be thronged with devout worshippers every Friday at noon, for public ritual prayers, and on other holy days; it can accommodate 25,000. These Friday prayers are compulsory for all adult male Muslims; before praying, believers congregate at the pool in the centre of the courtyard for the necessary ritual ablutions of hands and faces (above). From the minarets of the Jama Masjid the views across Old Delhi, to the north, and New Delhi, to the south, are among the most impressive in the city, and the cluster of bazaars around the mosque's base are typical of this crowded, bustling area.

New Delhi's spacious layout reflects the city's foundation as the British capital in 1911 and its adoption as the seat of government after Independence. The broad Rajpath, the 'king's way', runs from Rashtrapati Bhavan, the President's residence, to the India Gate (above right), the memorial to Indian soldiers who fell in the First World War, and is the setting for the annual Republic Day parade (opposite, below).

Other areas of the city bear witness to earlier times and older ways: elephants are still a form of transport (above left). Jai Singh's Jantar Mantar observatory (left) was built in 1725. The magnificent tomb of Humayan (opposite, above), the second Mughal emperor, is from the 16th century. Even earlier is the 13th-century Qutub Minar (top right), a gigantic Muslim victory tower on the outskirts of the city.

South-east of Delhi, on the western border of Uttar Pradesh, lies the city of Agra. This was the country's capital in the 16th and 17th centuries under the Mughal emperors Akbar, Jahangir and Shah Jahan, and is known the world over as the site of India's single most famous building, the Taj Mahal (opposite). Its story is still fascinating: it was commissioned by Shah Jahan as a mausoleum for his wife, Mumtaz Mahal, on her death in 1631; designed by a Persian architect, Isa Khan; the building and gardens took over 20 years to build by a force of thousands of workers, and Indian, Persian and Turkish master craftsmen added the fine decoration. Usurped by his son, Aurangzeb, Shah Jahan was imprisoned in the Red Fort on the west bank of the Yamuna river, from where he could see the Taj Mahal (left); on his death he was interred alongside Mumtaz. The Taj Mahal and its beautifully manicured gardens still provide employment for many (below right).

Upstream on the Yamuna is the enchanting tomb of Itimad-ud-Daulah, an important minister in the Mughal court of Jahangir and Shah Jahan (below left), set in a charming garden. This was the first Mughal building in India to be constructed of pure marble, and many of its features foreshadow those used in the Taj Mahal.

Agra and the surrounding areas are rich in sites associated with the Mughals. Agra's Red Fort (above) is a colossal city-within-a-city, begun as a defensive structure in 1526, and finished over a century later, by which time it was used as a palace. Its red sandstone walls are constructed in a crescent moon shape overlooking the Yamuna river, and encircle mosques, palaces and two halls, the Diwan-e-Am and Diwan-e-Khas. To the south-west of Agra lies the deserted city of Fatehpur Sikri (opposite, above); it was the Emperor Akbar's capital for 15 years in the late 16th century, after which the emphasis shifted to Agra, Delhi and Lahore, the three main capitals of the Mughals in the 17th century. Fatehpur Sikri's great mosque, approached through the Buland Darwaza gate (left), contains an important Sufi tomb or dargah.

Opposite, below: Another fine sandstone-and-marble Mughal complex is found at Sikandra, north-west of Agra; this houses Akbar's mausoleum, and has four elegant gates leading to the tomb.

The journey west from Agra takes one into Rajasthan. The eastern part of the state includes two of India's best-known wildlife sanctuaries. The Keoladeo National Park lies just to the south-east of Bharatpur, on the road to Jaipur, and is internationally famous as a breeding ground for over 120 bird species, such as Herons, Spoonbills (top left), *Ibis and Painted Storks (bottom left). Ranthambore National Park, south-east of Jaipur, is best known as the home of roaming tigers (centre left), and provides special protection to Asiatic tigers, whose numbers are decreasing every day.*

The hills around Rajasthan's state capital, Jaipur, are dominated by the great forts built by the Rajput princes. The oldest of these, Amber (above), stands on the Aravalli Hills to the north of Jaipur; it was begun in 1592 by Raja Man Singh, and was extended by later rulers. An ascent of the hills, on foot or by elephant-back, leads to a palace that contains both typical Rajput architecture and Mughal decoration: the most spectacular sight is the Sheesh Mahal (right), which was constructed in the 17th century. These private apartments of the Maharajas and their queens are decorated with a multitude of mosaics of small pieces of mirror and coloured glass, which create a uniquely dazzling, shimmering atmosphere.

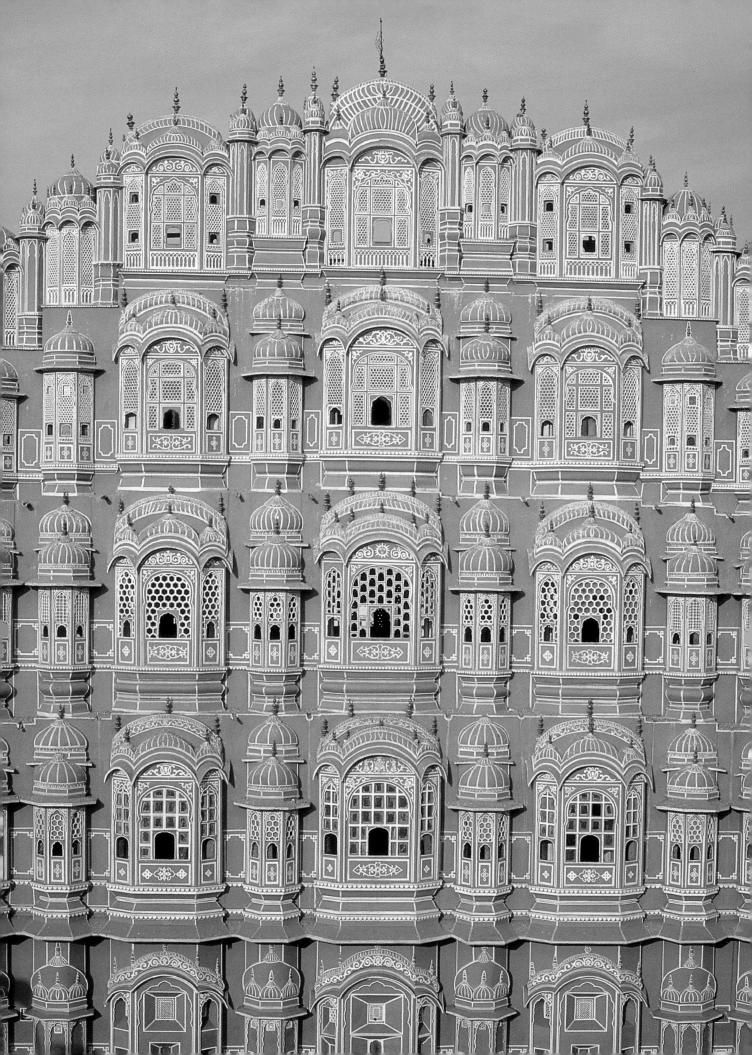

Jaipur was created in 1727 by Jai Singh, after whom it was named. The original city was laid out according to rules in the Hindu architectural treatise Shilpa Sashtra, *and was built in less than eight years. Its most striking feature is the pink wash applied to the buildings, giving Jaipur its universal title, the 'Pink City' – it was originally painted yellow, but the Rajasthani tradition of pink as the colour of hospitality was later adopted. Dominating the city centre is the imposing City Palace complex* (right); *although many of the buildings are open to the public, the royal family live in apartments in the complex, and the sight of turbanned and uniformed guards at the richly decorated doors* (above) *adds to the continuing tradition.*

Adjoining the Palace is the magnificent Hawa Mahal, the 'Palace of the Winds' (opposite), *in reality not much more than a façade, whose white-latticed windows and balconies enabled the women of the court, though in* purdah *(seclusion), to watch city life outside the palace walls.*

Although Jaipur is as bustling and busy as many other Indian cities, and enjoys its share of the tourist trade, its strictly planned layout has provided it with the advantages of more wide roads (above left) and public space than is often the case elsewhere. Looking down from the Hawa Mahal (left), as the court ladies once did, one can observe the activity in the street below. The camel-cart is as familiar a sight as cars and bicycles. The inhabitants of Jaipur are just as attractive as their Pink City, the Rajasthani men wearing coloured turbans and the women with bright veils and decorative jewellery (above right).

South-west of Jaipur, the landscape stretches into the desert, where towns such as Kishangarh and Ajmer dot the sandy hues with a splash of green. Barren though it is, this land has peace and a certain romance, exemplified by the timeless scene of camel-drivers trekking with their herds (opposite).

Although the small town of Pushkar is visited by pilgrims the year round – to worship at one of only two temples in India dedicated to Brahma – the main focus of attention comes during the full moon in October or November, when the Camel Fair is held. The fair is a great occasion for the Rajasthanis, whose traditional apparel is quite startling in its flamboyance, the men sporting huge, vivid turbans (above left).

Over 200,000 people and 50,000 camels, along with cattle and horses, arrive in and around Pushkar (right); *families come from all over Rajasthan and set up camps* (opposite, left), *and thousands of spectators* (above) *throng to watch the camel races.*

West of Pushkar, towards the Thar Desert, the landscape becomes drier and drier. Amid this stark countryside, on the edge of the desert, stands Jodhpur, the second largest city in Rajasthan. Founded in 1459, it is built around, and overshadowed by, the massive, dramatic Meherangarh Fort (above), which was constructed on the summit of a steep hill in the middle of the city. Close by is the white marble Jaswant Thada cenotaph, honouring a former Maharaja. This red-sandstone fort, the greatest in a state filled with hill forts, is entered by one of eight gates, and provides marvellous views of the old town, with its crowded bazaars, narrow streets and houses (left) Meherangarh Fort now houses a well-run museum for the royal collection.

Within the Meherangarh Fort, the palaces with their stone lattice-work façades (right) *evoke the glory and sumptuous life once enjoyed by the Rajput princes; they have descriptive names, such as Moti Mahal (Pearl Palace) and Sukh Mahal (Pleasure Palace). South-east across the city, the enormous Umaid Bhawan Palace is also constructed from sandstone, but has a very different history. It was begun in 1928 and, although the current Maharaja retains private apartments here, the rest has been turned into a luxury hotel and a museum of Jodhpur life. Although jodhpurs, the distinctive riding trousers, took their name from the city, they are rarely seen there now, except perhaps as part of the hotel doorman's uniform* (above right).

In the west of the Thar Desert, the unique town of Jaisalmer stands atop a hill rising from the sand dunes, crowned by its spectacular Fort (below), begun in 1156 by the Rajput ruler Rawal Jaisal. The honey-coloured yellow sandstone used exclusively for its construction gives the town its popular name of 'The Golden City'. The Fort's thick walls shelter nearly a quarter of Jaisalmer's population in a labyrinthine maze of small stone streets, and encircle bazaars, palaces and Jain temples. Jaisalmer grew in importance with the emergence of the trade routes between Central Asia and India. Newly wealthy local merchants used the local sandstone and wood to build fantastic havelis, tall mansions with courtyards in which every feature is beautifully carved and decorated in a Rajasthani style that reached its peak in Jaisalmer (left).

By far the most colourful and efficient way to explore the desert regions around Jaisalmer is by camel (above). Tourists can choose safaris and treks to historic sites and oasis villages, or just short rides among huge sand dunes in the vastness of the Thar Desert.

The many market sellers in the streets and alleys of Jaisalmer specialize in antiques, embroidered fabrics and shoes, rugs and carpets, just as their forebears have done for centuries in the ancient surroundings of the town in and around the Fort. In the Central Market (right) fruit and vegetable sellers spread out their wares in front of them on the ground.

All around Jaisalmer, the pace of life is unhurried and timeless. In the Thar Desert, shepherds take their flocks of sheep up the sand dunes of the Desert National Park (top), and Rajasthani musicians cluster round a harmonium player to perform traditional songs and tunes (above). In the rural desert villages, life has changed even less than in the town, and the sandstone walls and doorways are often painted in traditional Rajasthani designs (opposite).

To the north-east, the town of Bikaner, like Jaisalmer, has impressive havelis and temples. The window framing a palace guard (left) is faced with blue and white Delft tiles.

In contrast to its parched north-west, the southern part of Rajasthan is an area of cool lakes and green forests. The chief city in this region, Udaipur, is a delightful place with parks, museums and palaces, the largest of which is the City Palace (above) on the shores of Lake Pichola. This huge complex is filled with marvellously decorated buildings adorned with paintings and laid with tiles (opposite, above). Out on the lake, taking up the whole of Jagniwas Island, is the 18th-century Lake Palace (opposite, below), once a Maharana's summer home and now a luxury hotel. Udaipur's reputation as an artistic centre is also seen along its streets, where vivid paintings splash colour on house walls (left).

In most of Rajasthan, rural life continues in its old ways. In the remote wooded valleys of the Ranakpur region, north of Udaipur, teams of oxen trudge round a 'Persian wheel' used to raise water from village wells (opposite, above); women carry the water home in large jars balanced carefully on their heads (above).

Rural simplicity contrasts with the splendour of this region's Jain temples. The stunning Chaumuka Temple complex in Ranakpur (left), built in 1439, is one of India's largest Jain temples; its 29 marble halls are supported by over 1,400 pillars, each one different from all the others. Four other temples lie close by, in the shadow of the Aravalli Hills. Another spectacular series of Jain temples is located at Mount Abu, Rajasthan's only hill station, due west of Udaipur. The Dilwara complex comprises four temples entirely constructed from white marble; the oldest, Vimal Vasahi, was begun in 1031. Every interior surface is covered with intricate carvings, including the 48 pillars that support the roof in the front hall (opposite, below).

The ancient city of Gwalior, due south of Agra, lies near where the border of Rajasthan meets the north-western border of the state of Madhya Pradesh. Gwalior's Fort is in a spectacular position (above), on top of a sheer rock face. Much of the present Fort was built in the 14th century by the Rajput prince of the Tomar dynasty, Man Singh, who added fortifications and palaces inside the thick, solid walls. His most impressive achievement was the Man Singh Palace, with its intricate tile work and mosaics on the exterior walls (left).

On a journey south from Gwalior, the traveller is kept aware of the continuity of everyday life against the backdrop of history. At Sonagiri, women return from their work in the fields through the enormous archway of a Jain temple (opposite, below right), one of 84 shrines at this sacred site. Further south-east the palaces of Orchha, capital of the Bundela dynasty until the 18th century, are now deserted, except by tourists, but the inhabitants of the small village below the site are not concerned with departed splendours. The dhobiwallahs washing clothes in the Betwa river (opposite, above right) and the farmers winnowing grain (opposite, above left) have their own occupations to consider. Almost anywhere on this historic route, the traditional bullock cart, perhaps piled high with children (opposite, below left), is likely to be the most common sight.

The history of Sanchi, like that of Orchha, is one of decline from a vibrant city to a quiet village. Sanchi, near Bhopal, the capital of Madhya Pradesh, lies at the foot of a small hill in the mid-Indian plains; on the top of the hill rise several enormous Buddhist stupas, or funerary mounds, the oldest and largest of which, the Great Stupa, dates back to the 3rd century BC. *The site was founded by the Emperor Ashok on his conversion to Buddhism, and was added to by successive rulers until Sanchi boasted many temples, monasteries and smaller stupas. The Great Stupa is approached through four* torans, *gateways set at the points of the compass; the northern* toran *(above) is the best preserved and most elaborately carved. It is topped by a symbol of* dharma, *the law of life; further down, scenes from the Buddha's life and his miraculous works jostle for space with carved horses and elephants that support the main part of the gateway. With the decline of Buddhism in the region, which followed the rise of Islam in the medieval era, Sanchi was abandoned and forgotten until it was discovered by the British in 1818; it was only in 1912, however, that serious archaeological and restorative work was begun.*

Timeless India: herds of cattle (left) wend their peaceful way along a rural road near Orchha, in a scene unchanged down the centuries.

To Mumbai, Goa and the Western Ghats

The West of the Peninsula

Travelling to Mumbai (Bombay) and the historic riches of Maharashtra from the former princely kingdoms of Rajasthan, it is easy to bypass Gujarat; but this state in the far west has much of interest. Its north-western region meets the border with Pakistan and also touches Rajasthan across a vast area of flat, salty land known as the Rann of Kutch. The quiet rural lifestyle of the villages there is a great contrast to the industrial centre of Ahmedabad, the site of Gandhi's ashram, and the modern state capital named after him, Gandhinagar. In the south of Gujarat, the coastline is deeply riven by the Gulf of Cambay, which creates the Kathiawar Peninsula.

Western Gujarat is particularly associated with Jainism, as seen at the temples at Palitana and Junagadh on the Kathiawar Peninsula. On the mainland, the area around Baroda (Vadodara) is steeped in history, with medieval forts and many old temples and mosques. As one heads south into Maharashtra, two sites stand out: the marvellous 5th- to 8th-century Buddhist caves at Ajanta, carved out of the rock and painted on almost every surface, and the later cave-temples of Ellora, which are among the great wonders of the world.

Mumbai, the Maharashtran capital, is built on seven linked islands on the western coast of the peninsula. It was developed by the Portuguese in the 17th century, and then by the British. Mumbai is India's commercial centre. Also known as Bollywood, over 200 films are produced here each year, and huge billboards vie for attention with Victorian buildings and soaring skyscrapers.

The Western Ghats, the forested hills that run from north to south down the western side of the Indian peninsula, form a natural barrier between the tiny state of Goa and the interior. Goa's long stretches of white sandy beaches have kept it high on the list of favourite holiday destinations for years. This state's legacy of a 400-year Portuguese rule is seen in the many Catholic churches, but by contrast, many dynasties ruled what is now the state of Karnataka to the east of Goa, and their history is seen everywhere, from the ruined city of Vijayanagara in the north to the medieval Hoysala temples around Mysore in the south. Mysore itself is linked to the Hindu Wodeyar rulers, whose palaces still remain, sometimes as museums or luxury hotels. South of the city, extensive forested areas contain the wildlife parks of Bandipur, Madumalai and Nagarhole.

Bangalore, the capital of Karnataka, is a pre-eminent centre of industrial and high-technological development. To the south rise the beautiful Nilgiri Hills. Many of the slopes are covered with tea plantations, the principal activity around the charming former British hill station of Ootacamund (now Udagamandalam), where the houses and gardens of a bygone and more leisured era have scarcely changed.

The Kutch region of north-west Gujarat is one of India's least spoiled and most unchanged areas. Typical village houses in the Great Rann of Kutch feature thatched roofs and elaborate tribal wall paintings (opposite, above); the traditionally dressed and tattooed villagers practise local crafts, such as leatherwork and embroidery, and many produce distinctively patterned wall hangings (opposite, below).

Gujarat is home to some of India's rarest animals: the Wild Ass can be found in the Rann of Kutch, and Gir National Park, in the southern Kathiawar Peninsula, gives sanctuary to the last remaining Asiatic Lions (above and left). The males tend to have less luxurious manes than their African counterparts.

PREVIOUS PAGES
Page 92: Baga is just one of many resorts in Goa where white sands and warm seas prove irresistible to holidaymakers. Page 93: The Maharaja's Palace in Mysore is lit up by thousands of light bulbs at festival times and on Sunday nights.

Gujarat is rich in temples and monuments of many religions. From the small town of Palitana, at the foot of a steep hill in the east of the Kathiawar Peninsula, Jain pilgrims climb 3,000 steps, or are carried in doolis *(swing chairs)*, to reach the summit, on which stand over 850 sacred temples (above) *dating from the 16th century.*

Vadodara, the capital of the state of Vadodara before Independence, is a good centre from which to visit the area's forts, mosques and temples. The Lakshmi Vilas Palace (left) *is the most elaborately decorated of the many palaces in Vadodara.*

South-east of Gujarat lies the sprawling state of
Maharashtra. Although more than three-quarters of
its population is Hindu, a series of shelters,
dormitories and prayer halls hewn from solid rock in
the hills in the north of the state show that it was once
host to many religions. The 34 caves at Ellora (above
left) contain Buddhist, Jain and Hindu temples and
sculptures, created before AD 1000. One of the most
beautiful shrines is the 8th-century Buddhist
Viswakarma (above right), also known as the
Carpenter's Cave from the carved-stone imitations of
wooden rafters in the roof; an immense figure of the
Buddha dominates the cave. More than 30 hillside
shelters at Ajanta, to the north-east, had been
abandoned for several centuries when they were
rediscovered in 1819, by a group of British soldiers
boar-hunting in the hills above, who spotted carved
entrances not completely obscured by vegetation. The
glory of Ajanta is the astonishing series of wall
paintings, which date from around the 5th century
and depict the legends and lives of the Buddha. The
Bodhisattva Padmapani, seen holding a water-lily
(right), is an exquisitely executed example.

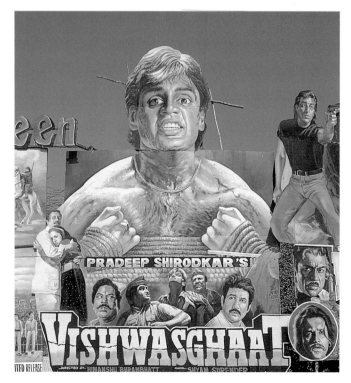

Mumbai is the capital of Maharashtra and India's most Westernized city. Top: Black-and-yellow taxicabs jostle for a space on the crowded roads. Left: A massive hoarding is a reminder of India's position as the world's most prolific producer of films. Above: The Taj Mahal Hotel has a reputation as the most luxurious hotel in India. Its modern tower-block wing dwarfs Mumbai's best known monument, the Gateway of India, built to commemorate King George V's visit in 1911.

Top: *A red double-decker bus passes Mumbai's busy Victoria Terminus railway station, now known as Chatrapati Shivaji Maharaj Terminus.* Right: *Office workers in Mumbai can have their lunch delivered by* dhabawallahs, *who each day distribute thousands of numbered and colour-coded tin boxes, packed with food at home and sent to the city's stations for collection.* Above: *Chowpatty Beach on Back Bay is a favourite place for relaxation, if not for bathing; here vendors sell snacks to visitors in the shadow of the tree-lined beach.*

Goa is a relatively new state, receiving the designation in 1987; it is also the smallest. For most people, Goa means stretches of beautiful tropical beaches. Along the coastline, from quiet Arambol in the north to Talpona in the south, coconut palms sway on the shores of the Arabian Sea and a stream of visitors comes to enjoy the relaxing atmosphere. Fruitsellers with refreshing basketloads (above left) and fishermen with their catch (left) are typically seen on many a Goan beach. Here they are at Colva, now one of the most popular resorts in the south and, as a result, becoming increasingly developed. Some quiet coves, such as Vagator (above right) have yet to be affected fully by mainstream tourism. The bright, white beach at Fort Aguada (opposite, below) is overlooked by the ruins of a 17th-century Portuguese hilltop fort.

In many of Goa's towns, the lively markets are a great attraction for visitors. One of the most famous is the weekly flea market in Anjuna, which specializes in arts and crafts such as wood carvings, batik work, jewellery and clothing. Many of the traders are tribal women (opposite, top left) *from other states. The multicoloured jackets strung in rows between palm trees* (below) *are often the work of women from Rajasthan and Andhra Pradesh who travel to Anjuna to sell their wares.*

The village of Mapusa, inland from Anjuna, holds a market where many traditional styles of textiles are bargained over (opposite, below), *while in the capital, Panaji (Panjim), a regular fruit, vegetable and provisions market* (opposite, top right) *keeps the local people well supplied. The Carnival festival in early spring brings a riot of colour, reminiscent of Mardi Gras, to Panaji's old city, as the Carnival King leads the revelry* (right).

Goa was a Portuguese colony from the early 16th century until 1961. The first Portuguese stronghold was Old Goa (top), along the Mandovi river from Panaji. Many great churches and seminaries were built there, before outbreaks of cholera and malaria caused the abandonment of the city in the 17th century. The most influential of the missionaries who came to Goa was St Francis Xavier, a founding father of the Jesuits; his body is interred in the Basilica of Bom Jesus (above), which was built in 1605. The largest church in Goa is the Sé Cathedral (left). All the Christian festivals are celebrated annually throughout Goa, such as this one at Calangute (opposite).

Karnataka, the state surrounding most of Goa, has had a turbulent history of rule by Buddhist, Hindu and Muslim dynasties, and their legacy remains in some of the most interesting sites in this part of peninsular India. East of Goa, the village of Hampi is overshadowed by the ruins of Vijayanagara, the huge capital of a succession of Hindu rulers until it was overrun and sacked by Muslims in 1526. Set in a landscape of tumbled boulders, the site spreads over a vast area; the Vitthala temple (left) displays astonishing workmanship in its wall friezes. Many of the finest temples are in the south of Karnataka, and were built by the Hoysala rulers, between the 12th and 13th centuries; these include Belur, Halebid and Somnathpur. Sravana-belagola is one of India's most ancient Jain centres, where priests regularly lay offerings at the feet of the 17m (55ft) statue of the naked figure of Lord Bahubali (above), built in the late 10th century.

On reaching Mysore, the traveller will know that this is truly the south, by the sights, the smells and the food. The city is one of India's major craft centres, renowned particularly for its sandalwood carvings, and is also known for its production of incense. The Devaraja Market, in the middle of the city, is nationally acclaimed and provides a real taste of southern India. Under awnings or in the open air, people stop to barter over the price of chillies (opposite, top), buy pan leaves (opposite, bottom left), or examine the explosion of coloured powders (opposite, bottom right) that Indians use to mark tikas on their foreheads.

Mysore was the capital of the state of Mysore until the latter became part of the newly named state of Karnataka in the 1950s. The city dates back to the 10th century, and was later ruled by the Hindu Wodeyar dynasty, whose history is mirrored in the many palaces around it; a number of these, such as the lovely white Lalitha Mahal Palace (left), have been turned into luxury hotels. To the south, Chamundi Hill offers views across the whole city, in particular of the Maharaja's Palace, also called the Amber Vilas Palace (above). This is a comparatively recent structure, erected in 1912. The interior of this huge building bewilders the eye with its extravagance: marbled stairways, tiled floors, stained glass, carved wood and vast chandeliers.

Mysore is rich in heritage; Bangalore, however, prides itself as being one of India's most go-ahead and growing cities. North-east of the former capital, it has a temperate climate and large, well-laid-out streets and parks. Although founded over 400 years ago, little remains of its earlier life as a fortress city, and much of the architecture dates from colonial days or later. The granite Vidhana Soudha (opposite, above), the seat of the Karnataka State Legislature, was purpose-built in 1954. The lions that grace the top of the dome, copied from the Ashokan column in Sarnath in Uttar Pradesh, are the emblem of the Indian Republic.

A banana lorry, delivering its load in Bangalore, strikes a cautionary note (opposite, below).

108

In the hills and forests of the southern peninsula some of India's finest national parks and sanctuaries have been established. Where the border of Karnataka meets the states of Kerala and Tamil Nadu, several adjoining protected areas shelter an abundance of wildlife. Elephants (left) and Gaur, the handsome Indian oxen, both have thriving populations in Nagarhole National Park. Adjacent are Bandipur National Park, Wynad Sanctuary and (above) Madumalai National Park, overlooked by the Nilgiri Hills, which is roamed by Tigers and Leopards, and is also rich in deer, monkeys, squirrels and birds. Visitors can arrange tours of these parks to view the wildlife and scenery.

Much of Karnataka's indigenous forest has been lost to modern development. Above: *Here, on a smaller scale, near Mysore, local people have cleared a tract for cultivation.*

Bandipur National Park is one of the areas designated a reserve under the government-initiated Project Tiger, which protects India's most celebrated animal. Right: *Grey Langurs are frequently seen in the park.*

Far right: *The wide-eyed Slender Loris is another jungle-dweller but, being shy and nocturnal, is rarely spotted.*

The southern parts of Karnataka and the northern fringes of Tamil Nadu have hill stations similar to those in the northern states; these were established by the British, whose influence is nowhere stronger than in Udagamandalam (Ootacamund), known universally as Ooty. This town in the Nilgiri Hills has churches, a racecourse and many small cottage gardens filled with delphiniums and roses. Many of the gracious colonial country houses have been converted into hotels but none is more luxurious than the Fernhill Palace (top left), *which was once the summer retreat of the Maharaja of Mysore. The nicest way to reach Ooty from the foothills to its south is to take the Blue Mountain Railway* (bottom left), *a miniature train that winds its way through the spectacular Nilgiris (the Blue Mountains).*

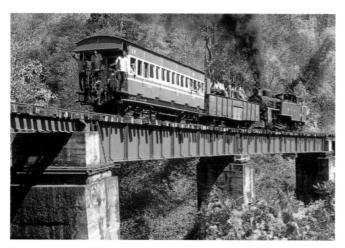

The principal source of revenue in the hills is tea, one of India's biggest agricultural industries. The great plantations around Ooty (above) *provide welcome local employment for pickers* (centre left) *and graders. The plantation manager's bungalow* (opposite) *has an 'English country' air, with its garden of roses and lavender bushes.*

TROPICAL WATERWAYS AND SOUTHERN CITIES

INDIA'S FAR SOUTH

The further south one travels down India, through Kerala and Tamil Nadu, the sharper the contrasts become with the rest of the subcontinent, especially the north. The pace of life becomes gentler and the climate grows ever hotter; sandy beaches and palm groves stretch into the distance. The people of Kerala, lithe and elegant, or of Tamil Nadu, whose dark complexions and often wavy hair betray their ancient Dravidian ancestry, dress lightly in *lungis*. Food in these mostly Hindu regions is vegetarian, and tropical fruits fill the market stalls.

Kerala's attractive coastal area, with its quiet fishing villages and lovely beaches, draws most visitors. Kovalam, a small sleepy town until about ten years ago, is one of the most popular resorts. Just travelling in the state is a novelty in itself, as the normal form of transport is by boat through the peaceful Kerala backwaters.

Christianity arrived on Kerala's Malabar Coast nearly 2,000 years ago and there is still a sizeable Christian population, mainly centred in the areas around the major port of Kochi (Cochin), which still has a scattering of churches. Inland from the Kerala coast, a green and tropical landscape rises into the highlands. In these regions, sanctuaries such as Periyar, and Annamalai in Tamil Nadu, protect wildlife.

India's most southerly point is reached at Kanya Kumari (Cape Comorin) on the very tip of Tamil Nadu. Here one of the finest natural sights in the subcontinent occurs during the full moon in April, when the setting sun and rising moon can be seen simultaneously. Turning back from the cape, the traveller can head north again to Tamil Nadu's temple cities. Nowhere else in India has such a concentration of monuments of the past. Huge complexes of soaring towers, enclosed by walls with great gateways or *gopurams*, dominate town after town: Madurai, Trichy (Tiruchirapalli), Tanjore (Thanjavur), and on through the heart of the state. Just outside Chennai, this history of south India's temple architecture had its birth in the wonderful 7th-century rock-cut shrines of Mahabalipuram.

Chennai, the capital of Tamil Nadu, is the fourth largest city in India; unlike Kolkota and Mumbai, however, it belies this by a comparatively less frenzied pace and mainly colonial architecture – the city was founded in 1639. For a reminder of the former French presence in India, Pondicherry (Puduchcheri), south on the coast, still has a Continental feel.

Some 1,190 kilometres (740 miles) to the east of Chennai, the Andaman and Nicobar Islands are the farthest-flung outpost of India. Despite their remoteness, the Andamans are becoming well known as a tropical paradise of white beaches and crystal clear waters. On the opposite side of the peninsula, off the Kerala coast, the island groups of Lakshadweep are sprinkled far out in the Arabian Sea.

Kochi (Cochin), which spreads over several islands, was founded as a port in the 14th century and in succession served the interests of Portuguese, Dutch and British traders. Above: The cantilevered Chinese fishing nets are just one example of the city's multiple foreign characteristics. Far left: Christianity was introduced to Kerala before it reached Europe, and Kochi's churches are still active. Left: Lake Vembanad separates the modern sector, Ernakulam, from the more historic areas of Fort Cochin and Mattancherry. Above right: Kathakali dance-drama is unique to Kerala, dating back over 500 years, and Kochi is well known as a centre for its performance. The brilliantly costumed dancers wear make-up made from natural ingredients (right), each colour a code for the character's attributes; green means purity.

PREVIOUS PAGES
Page 114: All types of boats are used on the backwaters and coastal lagoons of Kerala. Page 115: Candy-striped temple walls of the Brahmin village of Suchindrum abut onto the water.

Alapphuza (Alleppey) is the venue in mid-August for the annual Nehru Cup Snakeboat Races (above); the low dugout canoes, so called from their resemblance to a hooded cobra, are each crewed by about 50 to 100 oarsmen, and are cheered on by thousands of spectators.

South of Kochi, the backwaters of Kerala form a network of canals, rivers, lakes and lagoons between Alappuzha and Kollam (Quilon). All along the banks run small paths lined with palms (left); thatched huts (opposite, below) cluster at the water's edge, and people are busy with their daily lives. All manner of craft ply the waters, transporting logs (opposite, above), taking locals to and from their homes, and carrying tourists.

Thiruvanathapuram (Trivandrum), the capital of Kerala, is situated in the very south of the state, standing on seven hills facing the Lakshadweep Sea. Despite its official importance it has a relaxed atmosphere and low-key architecture; one of the few large buildings, the 18th-century Shree Padmanabhaswamy Temple, which is open only to Hindus, towers over low houses with red-tiled roofs (above right). The coffee houses (above left) are splendid and such establishments are a focus of social life throughout the state; although India is often thought of as a tea-drinking country, coffee is far more popular in the south. Trivandrum celebrates the twice-yearly Hindu Arat festival, dedicated to the god Padmanabhaswamy, with a parade of elaborately decorated elephants (right), which make their stately way to Shankhamukham Beach.

Opposite: Travellers arriving at the city's main long-distance bus station will alight under the swaying fronds of palm trees.

The south-western coast of Kerala is blessed with beaches of golden-white sand, broken only by rocky outcrops. Above: *Kovalam, in the far south, is growing in popularity as a tourist resort and Lighthouse Beach is regarded as the best holiday beach in Kerala. For local people, however, the sea is often their livelihood, and south of Kochi the principal activity is fishing.* Above right: *Fishermen haul in their nets at Varkala.* Centre right: *Small fishing villages, shaded by palm trees, dot the coastline.* Opposite below: *South of Thiruvanathapuram traditional fishing boats, some made from mango wood, still put out to sea, though motorized boats are becoming more widely used.*

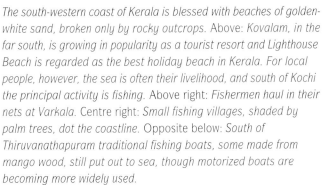

Right: *Just over the border, in Tamil Nadu, outriggers scud past Kanya Kumari, the very tip of the Indian peninsula, where the Arabian Sea, the Bay of Bengal and the Indian Ocean meet.*

In Kerala's tropical, green and hilly hinterland, several reserves have been established to protect the region's wildlife. The largest of these, indeed, one of the largest in the subcontinent, is the Periyar National Park, set in the Cardamom Hills on the border with Tamil Nadu. Boat trips on its huge man-made lake (left) are popular with visitors hoping for a glimpse of Periyar's many large animal species, which include Tiger, Leopard and Elephant (below), but in reality a guided tour on foot offers the best chance.

Also in the Cardamom Hills or Coramandel Hills (above), *but to the north near Pollachi in Tamil Nadu, the Annamalai Wildlife Sanctuary is mostly visited for its elephants and is important as one of the few remaining places where the rare Lion-tailed Macaque monkey can be found. The Parambikulam Dam, in the middle of the verdant forests, provides water for much of Kerala and northern Tamil Nadu. Clearings mark Malasar tribal villages (right), whose inhabitants still follow traditional ways of life in harmony with their surroundings.*

The historic city of Madurai was largely created by rulers of the Nayak dynasty. Its fantastic 17th-century Shree Meenakshi Temple is dedicated to the goddess Meenakshi, and every year devotees come here to celebrate her marriage with Shiva. Within the temple complex is the beautiful Golden Lotus water tank (above), which is surrounded by a superb colonnade and overlooked by the looming height of one of the gopurams or gates in the outer wall.

The Natraj Temple at Chidambaram, south of Puduchcheri, is dedicated to Shiva in his manifestation as the Cosmic Dancer (Natraj) and the walls and gopurams are decorated with dancers and musicians. The temple is maintained by Brahmins (left).

Tamil Nadu's great temples are a monumental history not only of Hindu architecture but of Hindu beliefs. As devotees offered more and more to their gods, so simple shrines became places of importance; with wealthy patronage, new features were built and the temple complex grew. By the 13th century the temple had become the very heart of the city, with boundary walls to contain its precincts. Today, as in the past, these walls are surrounded by traders, craftsmen, food stalls and flower-sellers (above), who cater for the worshippers and pilgrims.

The Chola kings, who ruled much of southern India between the 9th and 12th centuries, built one of the greatest of all temples, Brihadeshvara (above right), at Thanjavur. Its gigantic tower, topped with a golden finial, soars up 66m (216ft), an incredible feat of construction and architecture which was never to be out-rivalled. The surrounding wall is covered with skilfully executed sculptural representations of Shiva's attendants (right).

Chennai (formerly Madras), the capital of Tamil Nadu, grew in importance under the auspices of the the British East India Company, and its colonial past is still much in evidence. Fort St George (top) was first built in the 1650s, though very little remains of the original construction.

To the south of Chennai is Mahabalipuram, where the Shore Temple (left) stands right at the water's edge on the Bay of Bengal. There are also rock-cut shrines and a remarkable relief (above) sculpted across two gigantic boulders: Arjuna's Penance *is an allegorical representation of the descent of the Ganga to earth.*

Cooling breezes from the Bay of Bengal attract women and children to the beaches of Chennai (top); *rainbow colours and flowers in the hair are typical of the colourful dress of Tamil Nadu. The Fish Market* (right) *sells fresh produce from the Bay. On a city street, bicycle rickshaws await customers* (above).

India's two groups of tropical islands lie off the peninsula's southern coasts: to the west of Kerala, the islands of Lakshadweep and to the east, far out in the Bay of Bengal, the archipelago of the Andaman and Nicobar Islands. Not all of the Lakshadweep group are inhabited, some are mere dots in the ocean. The Andamans have for centuries been home to various indigenous tribes. Now the towns have grown and the tourist industry has recognized the potential of this tropical paradise, with its white beaches, unpolluted waters and surrounding coral reefs that are so tempting to divers and snorkellers. Havelock Island, reached by ferry from the capital, Port Blair, has a few fishing villages on the mangrove-strewn shores (left) and some quiet accommodation for visitors looking for peace and relaxation. The best place to swim is off the unspoilt beach at Radha Nagar (top). Wandoor (above) on South Andaman Island, is the starting point for a boat tour of the Mahatma Gandhi National Marine Park, which protects the habitat, waters and coral reefs of a number of enchanting islands.

From the Eastern Ghats to Historic Kolkota

The East of the Peninsula

From Chennai, the enormously long coastline of Andhra Pradesh stretches up the eastern side of peninsular India to Orissa. Inland, this large state sprawls from the low walls of the Eastern Ghats to the central Indian plateau of the Deccan. It was originally a stronghold of Buddhism, and excavations at Amaravati and Nagarjunakonda have revealed the

extensive remains of religious settlements, with monasteries and shrines that date back to the 2nd century.

Throughout later centuries, Andhra Pradesh was the scene of turbulent rivalry between Hindu and Muslim dynasties, whose monuments stand in testimony to the fluctuating fortunes of successive rulers. The 10th-century Venkateshwara Temple at Tirupati is one of India's most important centres for Hindu pilgrims; and just outside the state capital of Hyderabad, the formidable Golconda Fort, still impressive even in ruin, is a reminder of the might of Islamic kings in the 16th century.

Orissa, north-east of Andhra Pradesh, is a largely rural state with thousands of paddy fields chequering the fertile plains that lie between its beautiful coastline and the forested hills of the Eastern Ghats. These hills are home to over 60 tribal groups, whose culture and way of life have hardly changed in centuries. Bhubaneshwar, the state capital, has over 100 temples representing the peak of Orissa architecture. Two other outstanding Hindu temple sites are

easily accessible from the city: the Temple of the Sun at Konarak, designed as a huge stone chariot drawn by seven horses, and the sacred Temple of Jagannath at Puri, a magnet for devout Hindus and the starting point for a colourful and vibrant annual festival. Puri is also known for its lovely beach.

Inland, especially in Orissa's remote and beautiful forests to the north-east, there are several wildlife reserves. Heading across the eastern border into the neighbouring state of Madhya Pradesh, one can visit some of India's largest and most important national parks. Both Bandhavgarh and Kanha are famous as Tiger reserves, and are renowned for their abundance of other wildlife.

To the north of Orissa, on the banks of the Hooghly river, lies Kolkota (formerly known as Calcutta), capital of West Bengal. Founded by the British East India Company at the end of the 17th century, this is the second largest city in India after Mumbai, even though it no longer has the political and commercial dominance of the past. Despite the inevitable problems caused by over-population, Kolkota is not without its attractions and is famous as the centre of the lively and flourishing Bengali culture, which has produced writers, poets, filmmakers and playwrights. From Kolkota, West Bengal starts to leave peninsular India behind, narrowing and winding north towards the Himalayas.

The state capital of Andhra Pradesh, Hyderabad, was in the medieval era the seat of the Islamic Qutub Shahi kings. One of their outstanding landmarks is the 16th-century Charminar Gate (opposite). At Golconda, the ruins of the gigantic Golconda Fort (top) surround a rock-strewn hilltop overlooking the Qutub Shahi tombs. Hyderabad still retains a considerable Muslim presence (above). Pre-Islamic sites have been excavated at Amaravati and Nagarjunakonda (left), where statues of the Buddha still stand.

PREVIOUS PAGES
Page 132: Palm trees silhouetted against the sunset on the coast of Orissa. Page 133: On the beach at Puri, in Orissa, women collect the day's catch of fish.

Most travellers go to Orissa to see the famous temples of Bhubaneshwar, Konarak and Puri, which all stand within one comparatively small area. The enormous Temple of the Sun at Konarak (above), on the coast of the Bay of Bengal, is perhaps one of the most impressive. It dates from the 13th century and was built by the Hindu king Narasimhadeva as a monument to his success in repelling Muslim invaders; in the late 15th century, however, Konarak was taken and pillaged by Muslim armies, and over the years its great tower collapsed, and sand and rubble covered most of the rest of the structure. It was only in the early 20th century that archaeologists unearthed and began to restore the stone temple, which is constructed in the form of the processional chariot of the god Surya. There are 12 stone wheels along the base, and the chariot is pulled by seven horses.

There are carvings everywhere at Konarak, from the minute to the massive, and each of the three statues of Surya (left) is sited to receive the sun at different times of day.

136

A little further down the coast from Konarak, the temple of Lord Jagannath at Puri is one of several sacred Hindu sites, and throughout the year, pilgrims come from all over the country to worship at the wooden statues of Jagannath and his brother and sister. Each June or July, Rath Yatra, one of India's most important and spectacular festivals, is held, and thousands of temple attendants are used to build and decorate three enormous raths or cars (above). Each statue is placed in a car, which is then pulled by thousands of devotees down Grand Road to the temple at Gundicha Mandir. In the past, devout Hindus would throw themselves under the wheels of the raths, to achieve a holy death.

To the north of Puri, the numerous temples of Orissa's capital, Bhubaneshwar, are dwarfed by the tower of the Lingaraja Mandir temple (right), which combines power and grace in a massive stone superstructure, curving gently inwards in successive layers as it reaches its pinnacle at 36.5m (120ft).

A journey through rural Orissa, where the economy is primarily based on rice-growing, affords a fascinating insight into traditional lifestyles and culture. Often struggling against the vagaries of the climate, with flooding in the monsoon season, periods of drought, and sometimes more violent weather drawn in from the sea, small farmers use traditional wells to draw water (above) for irrigating paddy fields.

On the coast, fishing (opposite) is important to local villagers and in resort towns like Puri, tourists can enjoy superb seafood. Occasionally, unlucky turtles (left), though protected by law against being fished, are found stranded on the beach or entangled accidentally in a net.

Moving inland from Orissa, one enters the very heart of India and the state of Madhya Pradesh. Here in the central plain are two of India's finest national parks, Kanha and Bandhavgarh. The latter contains the ruins of a fort dating from the 1st century and a number of rock-cut cliff shrines. Humans are still settled in Kanha, among them communities of the Baiga tribe (left).

Kanha is best known as a Tiger Reserve, but it also has the occasional Leopard, monkeys, birds and several species of deer, including the graceful Chital, *or* Spotted Deer (below), *which can be seen wandering through open grasslands and along the forest edge.*

Tigers in Kanha (above) enjoy the protection provided by the park's status as one of the initial areas to come under Project Tiger. They are even becoming accustomed to the presence of tourists, to the extent that daylight sightings of this most glorious of beasts are no longer such a rarity as might be expected.

Bandhavgarh, too, has its Tiger population, as well as bears, wild boar, wild dogs, deer and an impressive list of birds. This park is particularly interesting for its remarkable scenery, which includes high rocky cliffs with an impressive fort and extensive areas of deciduous woodland (right).

Kolkota, the largest city on India's eastern seaboard, is situated at the point where the subcontinent starts to narrow into the triangular southern peninsula. It is the capital of West Bengal, a state that crosses the climatic barrier from the steamy heat of the plains to the cool air of the Himalayan hill towns. Kolkota is full of life and bustle, verging on the chaotic as traditional occupations rub shoulders with ultra-modern industries. Every day, its streets throng with people waiting to board crowded buses (opposite, above) or stopping at the flower market in the shadow of the massive Howrah Bridge (opposite, below left) on their way to or from work; the Vidyasagar Bridge over the Hooghly river to the south (above) was designed to relieve the Howrah, and was completed in 1992. The vast maidan, in which the Victoria Memorial is the backdrop to a game of polo (opposite, below right), was cleared from jungle to provide a clear field of cannon fire from nearby Fort William. South of Kolkota, the Hooghly flows into the Ganga Delta, where a coastal trading boat sails calmly along the West Bengal coast (right).

HIMALAYAN OUTPOSTS AND HILL STATES

NORTH-EASTERN INDIA

In the north-east of India, joined to the rest of the country only by the final narrow thread of West Bengal, seven states cluster at the eastern end of the Himalayas: Arunachal Pradesh, Assam, Manipur, Meghalaya, Mizoram, Nagaland and Tripura. To their west, separated from them by Bhutan, is the tiny state of Sikkim. The cool air, glorious green hills and spectacular scenery of these regions encouraged British administrators, sweltering in the heat of Kolkota, to establish their eastern hill stations here.

Darjeeling, in the extreme north of West Bengal, sets the scene, with its stunning views of snowy Himalayan peaks looming beyond the fertile surrounding countryside, blanketed by tea plantations. The town is a popular starting point for treks along the nearby Singhalila Ridge and further afield. Tiger Hill, a short distance from Darjeeling, is a favoured vantage point for watching dawn break over the summit of the mighty Kanchenjunga.

Remote Sikkim, once an independent kingdom, is an incredibly beautiful land of towering mountain peaks, forests filled with rhododendrons and orchids, rich orchards and magnificent Buddhist monasteries perched on hill slopes. Two of the most colourful monasteries, Rumtek and Phodong, are within easy reach of the capital, Gangtok.

Assam is world famous for its tea, but is also the producer of fine silks and a significant proportion of India's oil. Despite clearance of land for tea plantations, the state has retained some of its original forests. Two of its wildlife parks, Kaziranga, on the banks of the great Brahmaputra river, and Manas, are among the most important in India, not least for sheltering the endangered One-horned Rhinoceros. To the north of Assam, the large state of Arunachal Pradesh is home to over 50 different tribes, who still maintain their distinctive cultures in secluded valleys that split the high mountain ridges. Adjoining Myanmar (Burma), Manipur is predominantly a Hindu state and the centre for one of India's major classical dance forms. Its capital, Imphal, is the site of the world's largest daily market, where thousands of women gather each day to buy and sell wares. The immense Loktak Lake, to the south of the city, is unique for its 'floating islands' created by local fishermen and also forms part of the Keibul Lamjao National Park where, in an area of swampy marshland, the rarest deer in the world has its only refuge.

Meghalaya's population are mainly tribal peoples. Shillong, the capital, was once a British resort, chosen for its superb situation amongst pine-clad hills. Nagaland, the furthest north-east of these hill states and possibly the remotest, takes its name from the indigenous Naga people, legendary throughout this part of India as a warrior tribe.

In the foothills of the Himalayas, overlooked by the white peaks of Kanchenjunga (above), *the British established the hill station of Darjeeling* (left) *in the mid-19th century, as a refuge from the heat of the plains. The town is reached by the famous narrow-gauge 'toy train' from New Jalpaiguri* (opposite, above) *which winds its way north through the hills. A small number of Tibetans* (opposite, below right) *have settled in the town. Many Nepalese people come to Darjeeling to work as tea pickers* (opposite, below left) *in the huge plantations around the town.*

PREVIOUS PAGES
Page 144: *Silk-cotton tree blooms lie across a track in Kaziranga National Park, Assam.*
Page 145: *A demon image grimaces in Darjeeling's Aloo Bari monastery.*

The tiny state of Sikkim, formerly an independent kingdom, contains within its northern regions some of the highest peaks in the Himalayas, including Kanchenjunga, the third highest mountain in the world. Sikkim's neighbours, Nepal to the west and Tibet to the east, define the state's art and culture. The capital, Gangtok, has largely been redeveloped and has lost much of its traditional atmosphere, but the central market (above) is lively and crowded.

Sikkim's countryside is wild and beautiful, with rivers, deep valleys and forest-clad slopes. In spring, rhododendrons and orchids bloom. Trekking is permitted in some areas and visitors may have the chance to see the wildlife of the Himalayas, such as the delightful little Red Panda (left).

148

One of Sikkim's main attractions to visitors is the number of Tibetan Buddhist shrines (above), temples and monasteries set in spectacular positions among hills and valleys. To the north of Gangtok are the monasteries at Labrang, Phodong and Phensang, while to the west the gompa at Rumtek has become a favourite destination. Although this monastery was founded in the early 18th century by the Kagyupa order of Buddhists, it was extensively rebuilt in the 1960s, following an earthquake. The brightly painted main doorway (right) with its surrounding murals gives a foretaste of the highly ornate interior.

149

Assam, the largest state in the north-eastern region, supplies over half the tea grown in India and the hills around the tributaries of the wide Brahmaputra river that flows through the state are covered by plantations (above). *The tea estates provide work for thousands of pickers* (opposite, below).

North-west of Assam's capital, Guwahati (Gauhati), adjacent to Bhutan, the Manas National Park is one of the few areas where the rare One-horned Rhinoceros may still be found. Other animals in Manas include Tiger, the Pigmy Hog and a rare group of Golden Langurs (above right). *With luck, a visitor may catch sight of some of these inhabitants from the verandahs of the park's rest house* (right).

The Manas National Park (top) is home to herds of wild Elephant, but the cooling waters of the Manas river are also enjoyed by their domesticated counterparts (opposite), which are widely used in the region for transporting tourists and working in the forests. Birdlife in Manas is varied and abundant. One of the most impressive species is the Great Pied Hornbill (above left), the largest of several Indian hornbills, with its massive casque-topped bill. Like Manas, the equally important Kaziranga National Park to the east shelters the largest population of One-horned Rhinoceros (above right), which is closely protected.

Although Arunachal Pradesh is now coming into closer contact with the modern world, this long-isolated state is still firmly attached to its cultural roots. Among its indigenous tribal peoples are the Apatanis (top) of the central region. The nose-plugs worn by Apatani women as tribal identification (above left) are rarely seen today, but the podum, or top-knot, is still worn by most men (above right) – though, here, the traditional style of bound hair secured with a brass skewer has been updated with a knitting needle and wool. The bamboo bridge (left) is typical of the region, but similar constructions can be seen all over the state.

Arunachal's tribes are each distinguished by individual styles of clothing and decorations, nearly all of which have cultural or social significance. Top right: *The war headgear of a Tajun man is splendidly adorned with hornbill feathers.* Top left: *This Nishi headman, too, wears hornbill feathers in his hat. His red coat continues a tradition started when British administrators gave headmen red coats to mark their status.* Above: *Like all the men of his tribe, this Tajun village elder wears a turquoise necklace, while his wife also conforms to custom with the cropped hairstyle traditional among the tribe's women.* Right: *The fur hat and leopard's claws are typical of a Hill Miri tribesman. His pipe and woven basket are both made of bamboo.*

The state of Manipur lies next door to Myanmar (Burma). A Buddhist area in early times, it later came under the influence of Hinduism, which brought in its wake the dance and music that developed into the unique Manipuri form. In Imphal, the capital, the Jawarharlal Nehru Dance Academy is famous as a school of classical dance and the venue for performances. The graceful Ras dance has five main forms, all associated with the understanding of the divine nature of Krishna. The female dancers dress in stiff, embroidered and sequinned skirts (above left); every movement of the body is significant (left), and performers train for years to perfect their technique.

Near Imphal, the town of Moirang holds a festival every May, between spring and the start of the monsoon, to honour the pre-Hindu deity Thangjing, to whom the ancient temple here is dedicated. This is an occasion for processions (opposite, below left) and the Lai Haroaba dance, performed by both men and women, to the accompaniment of traditional music (top right).

Imphal is set on a flat plain surrounded by tree-covered hills. The city was founded in the lst century but, apart from its ruined Palace and the gold-domed Shree Govindjee temple to the east, there are few monuments to the past. Much of the centre of Imphal is occupied by the Women's Market (right), the largest daily market in the world, where over 3,000 women come every day to buy and sell food and household provisions. The casual shopper can enjoy wandering through the enormous covered aisles, stopping to browse over stalls offering local handicrafts, brassware and textiles.

Around the wide, flat streets of Imphal, bicycle rickshaws (below right) are commonly used for transporting goods as well as passengers, and the behatted cyclists can often be seen pedalling in front of what look like impossibly heavy loads.

To the south of Imphal is the vast Loktak Lake (left), where local fishermen have covered the waters with their unique 'fishing circles'. These floating islands are made of reeds and spiked around their perimeters with poles from which the fishing nets are suspended. Much of the fish caught in Loktak is sold at the daily Women's Market in the capital.

Part of Loktak Lake is within the boundaries of Keibul Lamjao National Park, a complex of wetlands (below left) that is the last home of the extremely rare Sangai, the Manipur race of the Brow-antlered Deer (below right). This is the most endangered deer species in the world and only a very small number remain, living in the floating swamps of the area.

Remote Nagaland, tucked in between Assam, Manipur and Myanmar (Burma), is the ancient home of the Nagas, who were regarded with awe throughout north-east India as a fierce warrior-tribe and even head-hunters. Their fearsome spears and painted war-shields (above) *bear out their reputation, but for the most part these people were, and still are, primarily agriculturalists.*

Meghalaya, a small state bounded by Assam to the north and west, and Bangladesh to the south, is one of the most rain-soaked parts of the world. The capital, Shillong (right), *centres on Ward Lake and is set amid hills and pine trees. Although its history goes back many hundreds of years, the present city was largely constructed by the British to be used as a hill station; the colonial Polo Ground is the setting for the annual archery stakes, and there is a decidedly Scottish influence in the tartan fabrics sold at the bustling bazaar stalls.*

ALONG THE HOLY GANGA

THE NORTH OF INDIA

The Ganga is the most sacred river in India, venerated since time immemorial for its life-sustaining properties. Down the ages, centres of pilgrimage were established all along its course through the northern states of the country, and holy cities, towns and temples rose on its banks. In the lands to either side stand milestones of India's oldest religions.

Pradesh – to Khajuraho. At this small village, a magnificent complex of Hindu and Jain temples represents the highest point of central Indian temple architecture and sculpture. The friezes and figures, often candidly erotic, that cover every surface of these wonderful buildings have few rivals for the exquisite craftsmanship and fine detail.

At Bodh Gaya, in Bihar, now marked by the splendid Mahabodhi Temple, the Buddha attained his enlightenment and from Sarnath, just outside Varanasi in Uttar Pradesh, he delivered the first of the sermons that were to spread his teachings throughout India. For Hindus, Varanasi, city of light and wisdom, is the holiest place in the world. Here, where the Ganga slows its pace in a wide curve, pilgrims and scholars have come for centuries to worship at the temples and bathe in the sacred waters from the endless flights of stone steps, the *ghats*, that line the river banks. Some 130 kilometres (80 miles) to the west, the city of Allahabad is sited where the Ganga meets its tributary, the Yamuna. Following a cycle of years, millions of pilgrims, among them the *sadhus* or wandering holy men, converge on Allahabad to attend the *melas*, religious festivals that celebrate this confluence, which has great importance in Hindu tradition.

Travellers following the route of cities along the Ganga want to turn south at Allahabad or Varanasi into Madhya

To the north of the Ganga, the capital of Uttar Pradesh, Lucknow, is interesting for its historic Muslim monuments and as a thriving centre of the arts. It is also one of the gateways to some of India's best-known national parks. Among them, Dudhwa, near Nepal and Corbett, in the foothills of the Himalayas, are havens for wildlife and both are Project Tiger reserves, Corbett being the first-ever established.

Where the Ganga narrows in its upper reaches, beyond the city of Haridwar, the forested hills that close in are scattered with religious sites. From here, thousands trek up into the beautiful Garhwal Himalayas region to enjoy the breathtaking mountain scenery. For many it is the start of a pilgrimage to the places that symbolize the very heart of their faith. Regardless of arduous trails, they journey to find spiritual fulfilment: at Hemkund, the glacial lake sacred to the Sikhs; at the Hindu temples of Kedarnath and Badrinath; at Gaumukh, where the Ganga, the Hindus' Mother Ganga, is born in an icy cavern in the 'land of the gods'.

For Buddhists, there is no more sacred place than *Bodh Gaya*, just south of the Ganga in Bihar state. *Here, 2,600 years ago, the young Buddha, searching for the meaning of life along the banks of the holy river, finally received enlightenment under the Bodhi Tree. The wonderful 19th-century Mahabodhi Temple that now marks the site of his awakening draws pilgrims from all over the world.* Above: *Youthful monks light devotional butter lamps at the shrine.* Left: *Further up the Ganga in Uttar Pradesh, just north of Varanasi, the Dhamek Stupa at Sarnath celebrates the spot where the Buddha gave his first sermon.*

PREVIOUS PAGES
Page 160: Pilgrims at Varanasi descend the ghats to bathe in the holy Ganga. Page 161: Fire dancers whirl their blazing torches in a spectacular performance at a Varanasi festival.

Varanasi, the holiest city in the world for Hindus, lies on the west bank of the Ganga. In the early morning light (above), the slow-moving river, with its ghats, boats and waterside buildings, presents a scene of tranquillity, soon to be shattered by the teeming bustle of humanity that fills the city every day. Pilgrims (right) arrive constantly from all over India and abroad, to bathe and perform devotions at the water's edge, and the narrow streets of the old part of Varanasi, too small for wheeled traffic, are always crowded with holy men, traders and onlookers. The city's many sacred buildings include the great 18th-century Golden Temple with its gilded spires, and the ochre-coloured Durga Temple of the same era, with its extra population of light-fingered monkeys. Across the Ganga, the 17th-century Ram Nagar Fort is still the home of the Maharajas of Benares (Varanasi's former name).

All along the west bank of the Ganga at Varanasi, seemingly endless flights of stone steps (ghats) – over 100 of them – run down to the water. Travelling from one to another is made easy by the boats that constantly ply up and down the river, transporting both pilgrims (top) and tourists. After bathing, fully clothed, the women change and hold out their delicate saris to dry in the sun (left). Sadhus, wandering ascetic Hindu holy men, are seen everywhere in the city (above).

For a Hindu, to die at Varanasi, or to have one's ashes committed to the holy Ganga, is to ensure release from the cycle of life and find immortality. Manikarnika (above) is Varanasi's most revered 'burning' ghat, where the dead are cremated and their remains given to the river to be carried towards the sea and a final resting place with their creator.

Upriver from Varanasi, the city of Allahabad is also sacred to Hindus as the meeting place of the Ganga and its tributary, the Yamuna, a confluence that has great religious significance. This joining of the waters is celebrated in the city by melas, or festivals, which in particular draw sadhus from all over the country to join in the processions (right). These men, who have foresworn all worldly encumbrances, lead the most austere of lives, constantly travelling on a personal journey towards spiritual wisdom.

To the west of Varanasi and Allahabad, and south of the Ganga, in the dry lands of Madhya Pradesh, the little village of Khajuraho is one of the most visited places in India. Over 20 Hindu and Jain temples stand here, dating back to the 10th and 11th centuries, all of them lavishly adorned with sculptural details of the highest craftsmanship. Largest and most imposing of these is the Kandariya Mahadev Temple (left), *dedicated to Shiva and belonging to the World Heritage Site complex, with several other temples. Its exquisite friezes depict scenes from the legends of the gods and court life, and many of them have a frank eroticism and sensuousness* (below right) *which shocked the Victorians who rediscovered the site in 1838 after centuries of neglect. Based on the same high platform that raises Kandariya Mahadev from the ground is one of several magnificent lion sculptures* (below left) *that appear throughout the complex.*

The Vishvanatha and Parvati Temples (opposite, below) *and the Parshvanatha Temple, which is among the Jain group in the east of the site and has been extensively renovated, are also profusely decorated with images of the gods and their consorts. Among the most enchanting sculptures at Parshvanatha are the portrayals of women in a variety of activities* (opposite, above).

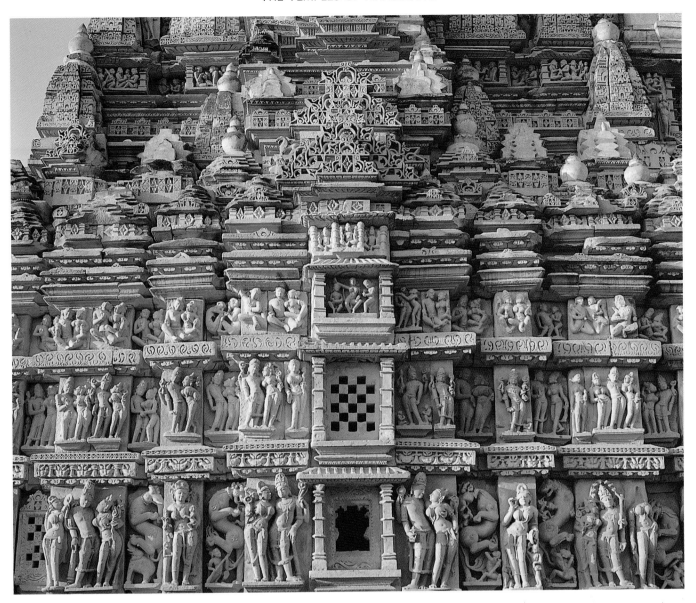

Following the line of the Ganga up through Uttar Pradesh, drawing ever nearer to the Himalayas, brings one to a series of superb wildlife sanctuaries. Dudhwa National Park, lying north of the Ganga, close to Nepal, is known for its numbers of Leopard and a fine population of Barasingha or Swamp Deer (above), which frequent the extensive grassy areas among the park's forests. Corbett National Park, in the state of Uttaranchal, has the distinction of being the first park to be designated a reserve under Project Tiger. It was named after the hunter-naturalist, Jim Corbett, who as far back as the 1940s recognized the threats facing the Indian Tiger (left).

The best way to see Corbett National Park is on elephant back (above right). This park is one of the most scenically beautiful in India, spreading over hills and covered with dense tracts of forest that harbour a rich variety of wildlife, including wild Elephant, bears and deer. The Ramganga river (right) winding through Corbett was dammed to create a reservoir, and this has become a magnet to vast numbers of waterfowl. Its shores are the haunt of marsh crocodiles and the Gharial, a fish-eating crocodile.

Haridwar (above left), on the banks of the River Ganga in Uttaranchal, is one of the seven holy cities of Hinduism. For pilgrims, it marks the start of the final pathway to the abode of the gods among the sacred snows of the Himalayas; thousands come here to worship at its temples and bathe from the ghats. North-east of Haridwar, in the Garhwal region, the Ganga (left) becomes narrower. Among the forested hills are shrines and ashrams, such as those at Rishikesh and Devaprayag, where travellers in search of spiritual peace can stop to rest and pray.

In the far north of the Garhwal, there are many holy places high in the Himalayan foothills. Of especial importance to Sikhs (top) is a pilgrimage to the sacred glacial lake at Hemkund (above), described in their holy book, the Guru Granth Sahib. *Not far from Hemkund, the town of Badrinath (opposite) on the Alaknanda river, the main tributary of the Ganga, has for centuries drawn Hindu devotees to its temple and hot springs.*

Pilgrims arriving at the holy sites of the lower Himalayas will not only have reached their journey's end but have come as close as they may ever get to spiritual fulfilment. For here, surrounded not by massive ornate temples but by the pure air and sparkling peaks of the mountains, they are truly close to their gods. The trails that criss-cross this beautiful region can only be taken on foot or by pony; one can travel at peace with nature. From the small town of Gangotri (opposite, above), where snow-capped summits such as Shivling tower in the background (opposite, far left), the final stage of a pilgrimage for many Hindus is the arduous route to the Gangotri Glacier. At Gaumukh (the 'Cow's Face') (opposite, left), their holy river and symbol of life's passage, great Mother Ganga, has its source in a cavern. Sadhus and many other spiritual seekers are found travelling everywhere throughout the Garhwal area. They may find their quest fulfilled at the end of the steep track to Kedarnath (above right). The temple here (above) is one of the most important shrines to Shiva anywhere in India. For some, the source of the sacred Yamuna river, reached by a delightful trek from Yamunotri (right), is their chosen destination.

INDEX

PHOTOGRAPHIC ACKNOWLEDGEMENTS

The publishers extend their thanks to the following people who kindly loaned their photographs for inclusion in this book. With the exception of those listed below, the photographs in the book were taken by **Gerald Cubitt**.

Fredrik Arvidsson: pages 6, 23, 28 (right), 29, 30, 32, 33 (above left and below left), 34 (right), 35 (above left), 36, 41, 55 (below left and right), 61, 64 (below right), 66 (below left), 68 (above), 69 (below), 72, 75, 76 (below), 77 (above and below), 78 (above), 79 (above), 82 (below left), 87 (below), 91 (right), 93, 95 (above and below), 96 (above), 97 (above left and above right), 99 (above), 100 (below), 104 (above and below left), 106 (above and below), 121 (below), 126 (below), 127 (above right and below), 128 (all three subjects), 133, 134 (all three subjects), 135, 137 (below), 138 (above and below), 139, 160, 162 (above left)

Laurence Arvidsson-Pujol: page 103 (above)

Axiom (Jim Holmes): pages 51 (below right), 56 (above), 58 (below), 107 (below left and below right), 129 (above), 142 (below left), 146 (below), 147 (below right)

Tim Harvey: pages 22, 37 (below right), 44, 63 (above), 99 (below left and below right), 105, 112 (centre left), 113 (above and below), 129 (below right), 142 (below right)

Bruce Herrod: pages 19 (below left), 170 (above left), 171, 172 (below left and below right), 173 (above right and below)

Caroline Jones: pages 2, 33 (above right), 60, 65 (above), 83, 84 (above), 100 (above left)

Maurice Joseph: pages 11, 18 (below right), 28 (left), 39, 50 (below), 52 (above), 53 (left), 56 (below), 58 (above left), 59 (above), 73 (below), 76 (above left), 81 (below), 88 (above), 89 (all four subjects), 90, 101 (below), 102 (above left), 103 (below), 115, 116 (below left and below right), 117 (above right), 118 (left), 119 (above and below), 150 (above), 154 (below centre), 155 (above right, below left and below right), 156 (above right), 157 (above and below right), 158 (below right)

Norma Joseph: pages 3, 18 (above right), 19 (above and below right), 33 (below right), 57 (above and below), 64 (above right), 80 (above), 88 (below), 150 (below), 154 (above, below left and below right), 155 (above left), 156 (above left and below), 157 (below), 158 (above and below left), 159 (left), 161, 164 (below left)

Life File (Graham Buchan): pages 172 (above), 173 (above left); (Sue Davies): page 129 (below left); (Caroline Field): page 7; (Gina Green): page 35 (below); (Cecilia Innes): pages 64 (below left), 69 (above), 85 (above), 108 (below), 118 (right); (Lionel Moss): page 71 (above); (Richard Powers): pages 66 (above), 82 (below right), 85 (below), 98 (above), 109 (below), 123 (top right), 165 (below), 176; (Terence Waeland): page 74

(below)

Neil McAllister: pages 5, 10, 18 (below left), 21, 35 (above right), 37 (below left), 43 (below left and right), 45, 46 (below), 47, 62 (below), 63 (below), 64 (above left), 65 (below), 66 (below right), 81 (above), 84 (below), 98 (below left), 107 (above), 112 (top left), 123 (centre), 127 (above left), 130, 131 (above right and below right), 142 (above), 143 (above), 145, 147 (above), 162 (below), 163 (above and below), 164 (above and below right), 165 (above), 167 (below)

Lawrence Marshall: pages 59 (below), 112 (bottom left)

Charlotte Parry-Crooke: page 37 (above right)

Simon Reddy: pages 25, 38, 43 (above left), 92, 101 (above), 102 (above right and below), 109 (above), 116 (above), 117 (below), 120, 121 (above left and above right), 122 (above), 123 (bottom right)

Peter Ryan: pages 31, 73 (above)

Kamal Sahai: pages 17, 18 (above left), 24, 27, 137 (above)

Taj Group of Hotels: page 98 (below right)